*A*ircraft of the same model and configuration are only visually distinguishable by the markings carried, this paintwork serving to provide individual identities and, in the case of military machines, often unit assignment and tactical markings. Additionally, unofficial adornments are also sometimes applied by operating personnel. The paintwork, in fact, often

ABOVE: Only a handful of Mustangs in the 353rd FG boasted any camouflage paint, ace William Tanner's P-51D *Prudence 7th* (44-72212 LH-O) being one such aircraft. It had dark green applied to the uppersurfaces of the fin, tailplane and wings.

bestows to the inanimate an intangible property akin to personality. During the Second World War, the most varied and colourful aircraft markings were undoubtedly those of the United States Army Air Forces, providing a subject of fascinating complexity. This series of publications endeavours to cover all aspects of camouflage and markings as carried by the fighter aircraft types serving with the Eighth and Ninth Air Forces in the European Theatre of Operations (ETO) between 1942 and 1945.

The information provided in these studies not only offers the researcher a valuable reference source, and enables artists and modellers to make accurate representations of the aircraft operated by these forces, it also aids the identification of subjects in photographs. Known changes in aircraft markings can sometimes date a photograph to the day it was taken.

The photographs reproduced in these books have in the most part been selected to show particular markings in detail, and in the case of the P-51 Mustang, the variety of schemes is considerable.

Of the primary fighter types used by the USA in the ETO, the Mustang became the principle escort for heavy bombers. There were over 1,700 in service by the end of hostilities, the majority with the 14 fighter groups of the Eighth Air Force, and it is the decor of these units' Mustangs with which this publication is primarily concerned.

Roger A Freeman, January 2003

The P-51 Mustang and Derivatives

The Mustang, indisputably one of the most successful aircraft of the Second World War, was unsurpassed as a long-range single-seat fighter. The design originated from an approach in 1940 by the British Purchasing Commission to North American Aviation Inc to build Curtiss P-40s under licence. North American, offering to produce a better design within an exceptionally short time span, completed the prototype (designated the NA-73) in just 100 days. With favourable approval from the British purchasers, the NA-73 was put into production as the Mustang I, the first production deliveries being made late in 1941.

As the US Army Air Corps considered production of the Mustang 'foreign business', little interest was shown, apart from the acquisition of two experimental examples that were given the designation XP-51. Entering Royal Air Force (RAF) service early in 1942, the Mustang was employed as a tactical reconnaissance fighter for direct support of ground forces. Although the type had an excellent low-level performance, its Allison engine lacked the necessary supercharging for maintaining full power at high altitudes. As good high-altitude performance was imperative for successful combat with the current enemy fighter types encountered over north-west Europe at this date, the Mustang was relegated to the low-level tactical role, where its exceptional endurance proved a boon.

Although the RAF had no pressing requirement for a long-range fighter in 1942, primarily at the instigation of Rolls-Royce, a handful of Mustang Is had Merlin engines installed for experimental purposes. With the Merlin 60 series engine, the Mustang's high-altitude performance proved outstanding, leading to the installation of similar model Packard-built Merlins on the Mustang production lines during 1943.

To keep the production lines open after the first British purchases of Mustangs had been supplied, the United States Army Air Forces (USAAF) placed orders for limited numbers of Allison-engined P-51 models, notably the P-51A and A-36A, the latter being a dive-bomber version of the former. Influenced by RAF experience, the USAAF considered the type a tactical fighter that was to be employed in fighter-bomber or fighter-reconnaissance roles. The first production Merlin-powered Mustangs, designated the P-51B, were also to be assigned to tactical fighter units when sent to the UK in the autumn of 1943.

At this time, with the Eighth Air Force's daylight bombing campaign in crisis due to heavy losses, the need for a long-range fighter escort was imperative. However, the first P-51Bs had been sent to the Ninth Air Force, tasked with giving tactical air support to the land forces in the forthcoming cross-Channel invasion of Europe. As soon as the Eighth Air Force became aware of the Mustang's potential as a long-range fighter, it was given priority for the type.

With internal fuel tankage giving the P-51B a 400-mile radius of action, and with auxiliary 'drop' tanks extending this to over 600 miles, the Mustang at last offered the means of providing escort for B-17s and B-24s to and from any continental target they might attack.

Of the Ninth Air Force's three P-51B groups, one was transferred to the Eighth in exchange for a P-47 group and the other two flew under VIII Fighter Command control for some months. By February 1944 VIII Fighter Command had plans to convert all of its P-38 Lightning and P-47 Thunderbolt groups to P-51s, but the programme took 11 months to complete, such was the demand from other theatres of war for the Mustang.

The first UK arrivals

Early production P-51Bs were initially shipped to the UK during September-October 1943, and were scheduled to equip three Ninth Air Force fighter groups. As received, the Mustangs were painted in the then standard USAAF camouflage scheme of Dark Olive Drab (shade 41) uppersurfaces and Neutral Gray (shade 43) undersurfaces. The spinner was Dark Olive Drab.

Early production aircraft featured the first version of the 'star and bar' national insignia with a red surround, but most aircraft that reached the UK had the blue surround, or had this so painted before reaching squadrons. On the fuselage, the diameter of the central blue disc with the white star was 30 inches, centred 36 inches forward of station 248 (rear of the radiator section). On the upper left and lower right wing surfaces the national insignia was centred on station 166, located at the outward end of the trim tab, and approximately $55^{1}/_2$ inches from the wing tip. The diameter of the central device was 35 inches. The positioning and size of the national insignia on USAAF Merlin-engined Mustangs was consistent throughout the production runs at both North American Aviation factories producing P-51s, apart from the odd deviation in application. The standard Insignia Blue (shade 47) was noticeably lighter on some aircraft, and this was believed due to a variation in paint manufacture.

Individual aircraft data – model, serial number, crew weight and fuel-servicing – was applied in black $1^1/_2$-inch and inch high block characters on the left side of the fuselage just forward of the cockpit as standard USAAF practice. The serial number, less the leading 4 and hyphen, was repeated on both sides of the fin and rudder. Originally known as the 'radio call' number, and providing a more visual version of the serial, it later became generally known simply as the 'tail number'. Painted in Identification Yellow (shade 48), the numerals were eight inches high, with two-inch spacing. With five-digit tail numbers, two were stencilled onto the fin and three on the rudder. Six-digit numbers had three each on the fin and rudder. The tops of the numerals were two inches below a line taken from the bottom of the rudder trim tab.

The majority of instructional markings were in black inch high characters, a notable exception being the No Step with the red L-shaped device on the uppersurface of the left flap by the wing root fairing.

The 354th Fighter Group

The first of the three Ninth Air Force groups to be equipped with the P-51B, the 354th Fighter Group (FG) arrived in the UK at the beginning of November 1943. Its personnel had trained mostly on P-39 Airacobras, and few if any had flown P-51s in the USA, as had the pilots of the following groups, the 357th and 363rd, which arrived at the end of the year. The 354th, upon receiving its first aircraft at Greenham Common, in Berkshire, moved during the second week of November to Boxted, near Colchester in Essex, which became its combat station.

RIGHT AND BELOW: The only additional authorised markings painted on P-51Bs of the 354th FG before commencing operations were SD 110 squadron codes. These were white and 24 inches high, with the squadron code forward of the national insignia and the individual plane-in-squadron letter aft. The stencil breaks in GQ-M had yet to be painted over when this photograph was taken on the Boxted main runway on 15 December 1943. This P-51B was the assigned aircraft of Lt Charles Gumm, who the press would proclaim as the first Mustang ace in the ETO. Most of his victories were obtained in a later assigned aircraft marked GQ-V. Type identity bands were hurriedly added a few days later, and as the photograph of the tail shows, the positioning and dimensions of these bands were not always true to the directive.

By mid-November a system of unit markings had been devised whereby the aircraft of the group's 353rd, 355th and 356th FSs would be identified as A, B and C. Individual aircraft within each squadron were to be identified by different letters. The squadron and individual aircraft letters were painted together in light grey on the rear fuselage in approximately 15-inch high letters. However, this system was short-lived, and few aircraft actually had the letters applied. An example is 43-12488 of the 353rd FS, which carried the letters AM.

By the date of the 354th's introductory operation (a fighter sweep on 1 December 1943), Air Ministry SD 110 codes had been issued and applied. The 353rd FS's combination was FT, the 355th's GQ and the 356th's AJ.

As with the USAAF's P-47 Thunderbolts that were already operating in the UK, the Mustang's unit letters were painted in white 24-inch high block capitals forward of the national insignia on both sides of the fuselage. On P-51s, the horizontal panel line above the bar of the national insignia, and extending forward below the cockpit edge, was used as the upper limit in the application of the squadron letters. The individual plane-in-squadron letter was usually placed with the forward edge close to station 248 on both sides of the fuselage.

Mirroring the concern that the Thunderbolt would be mistaken for the Fw 190 because of its radial engine, there was a belief that a fighter with square cut wing tips might be erroneously identified as a Bf 109. Following a number of interceptions of P-51s by P-47 and P-38 pilots in the weeks following the 354th's introduction to combat operations over enemy territory, type identity markings were introduced similar to those used by RAF Mustangs in 1942.

As with Thunderbolts, white banding was applied to nose and tail surfaces, and additionally around each wing. Issued on 20 December 1943, the order specified the following application in white: propeller spinner and a 12-inch wide band encircling the nose directly aft; a 12-inch wide horizontal band around the fin and rudder, with the top edge 18 inches below the fin tip; a 15-inch wide band around each tailplane, centred 33 inches from the tips; and a 15-inch wide band around each wing approximately 15 ft from the tips, with the inner edge running against the main wheel cover. While some of the application work was performed 'in-the-field' by service squadrons, most was carried out at Base Air Depots before the aircraft were issued to front line units.

Silver Mustangs

The USAAF directive to manufacturers to discontinue camouflage paint was effected on the 770th P-51B airframe (serial 43-7083) at Inglewood, California, in December 1943. On this and all following aircraft, the tail number was painted in black. An area forward of the windshield extending forward to the spinner was painted olive drab as an anti-glare measure.

A second source of Merlin Mustang production, established in Dallas, Texas, in 1943, commenced deliveries of P-51C models, which were virtually identical to P-51Bs, in November of that year. The first 200 P-51Cs were accepted by the USAAF in a camouflage finish of Dark Olive Drab uppersurfaces and Neutral Gray undersurfaces, with tail numbers in yellow. With the delivery of aircraft serial 42-103179, camouflage finish was abandoned and tail numbers were applied in black.

The tail numbers of the first three blocks of P-51Cs were of seven digits, four being painted on the fin and three on the rudder. Spacing between the numerals was one inch. With a later batch of P-51Bs having seven-digit tail numbers (although four figures were painted on the fin and three on the rudder, as with the P-51C), the spacing between the figures was two inches. As P-51Cs had a down-rated engine, most of the Dallas-built aircraft were supplied to tactical reconnaissance units.

The arrival of P-51Bs in natural metal finish in February 1944 led to type identity markings being ordered in black. Meanwhile, adverse reports of the white band breaking up the distinctive square-cut shape of the Mustang's tail – an important recognition feature – led to an order issued on 23 March 1944 requiring the removal of this band. However, this only applied to Mustangs in camouflage finish, and the black band continued to be applied to the fin and rudder of unpainted aircraft. It is assumed that this marking did not have the same visually disruptive

BELOW AND BELOW RIGHT: Unpainted aircraft had black type identity bands, including that on the fin and rudder, which had been discontinued on the camouflage finish Mustangs. The seven-digit tail numbers had three figures on the rudder and four on the fin. Pierce McKennon's WD-A has finer code letters than Herbert Blanchfield's QP-E, showing that the different squadrons used different stencils. Both these red-nosed 4th FG 'silver' Mustangs failed to return from the mission of 9 May 1944.

effect when painted onto a 'silver' P-51. Code letters were also painted in black on bare metal finishes when these aircraft reached squadrons.

The first 'silver' Mustang to reach a combat unit in the UK was P-51B-1 serial 43-12437, which was declared unsuitable for combat use, and thereafter used for operational training by the 354th FG at Boxted. This particular Mustang's camouflage paint had been removed by groundcrewmen of the 356th FS at the fighter station early in February 1944, but shortly afterwards, on 10 March, the war-weary machine was destroyed in a fatal crash.

The First Eighth Air Force Mustangs

The first Mustang obtained by the Eighth Air Force was an RAF Mark I in which Rolls-Royce had installed a Merlin engine. Sent to Bovingdon, in Hertfordshire, for evaluation by VIII Fighter Command's Air Technical Section, it was given a standard USAAF camouflage scheme of Olive Drab and Neutral Gray and later the white type identity bands as well. Powered by a Merlin 65 and designated a Mustang X, the fighter's RAF serial (AM121) was painted on the fin in USAAF fashion, and the code VQ-R was applied on the fuselage in white.

BELOW: The 357th FG was equipped with Mustangs while stationed at Raydon, in Suffolk, with many of those received for flight experience being hand-me-downs from the 354th FG. P-51B 43-6370 was one of the first readied for operational use, coded G4-O.

The first Eighth Air Force P-51B fighter group, the 357th, was obtained from the Ninth Air Force in an exchange for the P-47-equipped 358th FG – the two groups exchanged bases at the end of January 1944, the 357th moving from Raydon to Leiston (both in Suffolk) and the 358th the reverse. At this time, the 354th FG, which had flown its first combat mission on 1 December 1943, was still operating under VIII Fighter Command control, and continued to do so for some time to come. The 357th FG Mustangs did not join the 354th on combat missions until 11 February 1944.

LEFT: This muddied P-51B of the 362nd FS/ 357th FG, was photographed in February 1944. It appears to have had part of its spinner painted black. During this month several fighter squadrons sported officially unapproved nose colours, and this particular unit is reported to have had a few aircraft adorned with yellow noses, while some in a sister squadron boasted red spinners.

The 357th's trio of squadrons – the 362nd, 363rd and 364th FSs – were identified by the codes G4, B6 and C5 respectively. These units were among the first USAAF squadrons to be issued with SD 110 Air Ministry codes which incorporated a numeral and a letter instead of two letters. This change was brought about by the large number of new squadrons entering service with both the RAF and USAAF in the UK, exhausting the available two-letter combinations. The 357th FG's squadrons painted their codes and individual aircraft letters in similar size and placement to 354th FG Mustangs, and in the process established a standard for all USAAF Mustangs with unit assignment in the ETO.

P-51B-5-NA 43-6437 of the 335th FS/4th FG, Debden, March 1944

Painted in the standard finish for P-51s prior to the introduction of bright colour markings, this aircraft was one of the original complement of Merlin Mustangs received by the 4th FG at Debden in late February 1944. Upon its arrival, 43-6437 was immediately acquired by the group commanding officer, Lt Col Donald Blakeslee, as his personal aircraft. It was given his favoured code markings WD-C, the C standing for 'Chief Cook', taken from the jovial accolade bestowed by the RAF on someone who was involved in all matters of responsibility, 'chief cook and bottle washer'. Don Blakeslee replaced this aircraft with new metal finish P-51B 42-106726 in mid-April 1944, and 43-6437 was in turn re-coded WD-V and used by other pilots. It crashed in France after being hit by ground fire whilst strafing on 7 August that same year, pilot Sydney Wadsworth being made a PoW.

RIGHT: One of the original batch of P-51Bs supplied to the 354th FS/355th FG, this aircraft featured *The Bulldogs* inscription above the exhaust stubs, as well as the nickname *MARJORIE II*. 43-7157 WR-S was received in an unpainted finish and then given a coat of olive drab or similar green from a British source at Steeple Morden. The trim tab is in a flight colour, believed to be red. This Mustang survived operations with the 355th and was later transferred to the 479th FG to serve in operational training. It went missing on 12 December 1944, believed lost in the North Sea whilst on a training flight with recently-arrived 435th FS pilot Lt Robert B Hymans at the controls.

By February 1944 the Eighth Air Force, having secured priority for Merlin-powered P-51s, was preparing to convert five P-47 groups to the type, starting with the 4th FG at Debden. The group's CO, Lt Col Don Blakeslee, had been loaned to the 354th FG to lead its introductory missions. He had been so taken with the Mustang's potential that he persuaded Maj Gen William Kepner, Commanding General of VIII Fighter Command, to let the 4th FG be the first to shed its P-47s for P-51s.

A valid point in favour of the 4th was that several of its pilots were ex-RAF 'Eagle Squadron' men who had Merlin engine experience flying Spitfires (see *American Eagles 1: American Volunteers in the RAF 1937-1943*). This fighter group undertook its first operation with Mustangs on 25 February 1944. Squadron code markings remained as carried on the P-47s, with the 334th FS using QP, the 335th WD and the 336th VF. The second Thunderbolt group to convert to the Mustang, the 355th FG, became operational in March 1944. Its three flying units were the 354th, 357th and 358th FSs, with codes WR, OS and YF respectively.

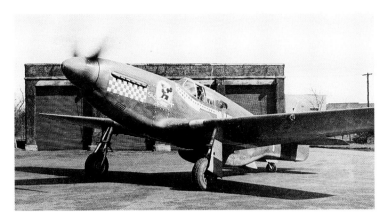

ABOVE AND ABOVE RIGHT: Capt Don Gentile's flamboyantly decorated P-51B 43-6913 VF-T of the 336th FS/4th FG. Named *Shangra-La*, it carried a block of red and white checkerboard on both sides of the nose below the exhaust manifold. John Godfrey, who often flew as Gentile's wingman, had a similar marking applied to his P-51B. The purpose of this duplication was, allegedly, so that both pilots could easily identify the others' aircraft during the heat of battle. Surprisingly, this embellishment was tolerated by higher command. The boxing eagle motif was the unofficial emblem of the 4th FG.

RIGHT: These black and white swastika symbols adorned 10.5-kill ace Lt Col James Clark's P-51B 43-6560 QP-W of the 334th FS/4th FG – the halved swastika indicates a victory shared with another pilot. The code letters (the letter Q is partially visible at lower right) on this aircraft have been picked out with black. This Mustang was lost to flak over Mackfitz airfield, in Poland, on 29 May 1944 while being flown by ground-strafing ace Lt Frank E Speer.

Bright colour markings

Early in February 1944, the P-47-equipped 56th FG had received permission to paint the noses of its aircraft in a different colour for each squadron. Other fighter units were not long in following suit, and by early March the 4th FG was painting the spinners and nose band of its Mustangs scarlet. A few 357th FG P-51s were also reported with yellow noses and bright colours similar in style to the markings that had appeared on P-47s and P-38s flown by other units.

The full extent of the unofficial application of bright colours on Eighth Air Force fighters during the latter part of February and early March 1944 is not known, but by mid-March VIII Fighter Command had called a halt. A plan was then developed to provide a group identity feature with different nose colours. As finally approved (although apparently incorrectly posted in some reports at the time), the groups of the 65th and 67th Fighter Wings were to use solid colours, and those of the 66th a checkerboard. On P-51s, this would involve the spinner and the 12-inch wide type identity band that encircled the nose, the latter divided into six-inch squares to form the checkerboard for the 66th Fighter Wing.

4th FG P-51s would continue to have red noses and 355th FG fighters white, while the black type identity nose band on bare metal aircraft was replaced by an identical marking in white. The 357th FG adorned its Mustangs with red and yellow checkers, with the spinner divided equally into three bands of red, yellow and red. Groups yet to convert were also assigned recognition colours – the 352nd FG blue, the 359th FG green and the 361st FG yellow. Finally, the newly arrived 339th FG, which had originally been scheduled for service with the Ninth Air Force but had been exchanged for the P-47 equipped 50th FG before its arrival in the UK, was to be assigned to the 66th Fighter Wing, and use red and white checkerboards.

The 352nd FG at Bodney, in Norfolk, which converted a squadron at a time to the Mustang from late March 1944, applied a bright sky blue shade to the noses of its P-51s. The replacement of the white 12-inch wide nose band with blue was found to provide insufficient contrast on aircraft in the camouflage finish,

BELOW: Duane Beeson's *BEE*, alias P-51B 43-6819 QP-B of the 334th FS/4th FG, was photographed at Debden on 12 April 1944. The small white cross above the wing root indicates that the aircraft has had a fuselage tank installed.

LEFT: The bright grass green nose on camouflaged 359th FG Mustangs showed up well against the dark olive drab as in this photograph of P-51B 43-6491. The white fin and rudder tail band has not been painted out despite it being May 1944. An Indian girl motif on the nose had still to be completed, and the aircraft would eventually receive the name *Wanna Honey*. The code letters CV-E have black outlines. This P-51B was lost in the North Sea with Elmer H Cater at the controls on 4 June 1944.

ABOVE AND LEFT: Two 339th FG P-51Bs that had to be 'bellied in'. Markings are very similar, apart from the squadron codes. D7-V 42-106882 was from the 503rd FS and 5Q-Q 42-106672 from the 504th FS. The band of red and white checkers varied in placement from aircraft to aircraft. For example, D7-V has a red square placed directly in front of the exhaust manifold, whilst 5Q-Q has the join between a red and a white square centred on the manifold.

P-51B-10-NA 42-106672 of the 504th FS/339th FG, Fowlmere, May 1944
Apart from a few early Olive Drab P-51Bs used for training, the 339th FG was the first
group to be completely equipped with bare metal finish Mustangs. Assigned to Luther
L Corbin, 42-106672 enjoyed only a short life in the front line. On 18 May 1944, Harvey
R Waymire was flying it when the fighter's engine failed, forcing him to belly land in a
wheat field near Chedburgh airfield, Suffolk – see the centre photograph on page 8. The P-
51 was so badly damaged in the landing that it was declared fit only for salvaging.

so the blue paintwork was extended back to a point approximately halfway below the exhaust
stacks and then swept up and back to the aircraft's windshield. Mustangs of the 352nd FG were
first used on a combat mission on 8 April 1944. Squadron codes were PE for the 328th FS, PZ
for the 486th and HO for the 487th.

The 359th FG at East Wretham, in Norfolk, initially used a bright apple green for the spinner
and nose band as had been previously employed on its P-47s. However, when the squadron's
complement of aircraft was predominantly in bare metal finish, a darker shade of green came
into use. The 361st and 339th FGs conformed to the nose colour directions, with the latter
having an eight-inch wide red band encircling the spinner approximately an inch forward of the
propeller blades. The remainder of the spinner was painted white.

The 359th FG flew its first P-51 mission on 5 May, and the coding of its 368th, 369th and
370th FSs was CV, IV and CS, respectively. The 361st FG, based at Bottisham, in
Cambridgeshire, became operational with Mustangs on 12 May, and its 374th, 375th and
376th FSs were identified by codes B7, E2 and E9 respectively. All five groups converting to
P-51s in the first half of 1944 used the same squadron codes as had been carried on their
P-47s. The 339th FG, comprised of the 503rd, 504th and 505th FS with SD 110 codes D7, 5Q
and 6N, respectively, flew its first mission from Fowlmere, in Cambridgeshire, on 30 April 1944.

BELOW: In late May 1944 the first P-51D models with cut down rear fuselage, upper decking and 180-degree vision 'bubble' cockpit canopies were received by units in the ETO. All were delivered in natural metal finish, but each showed variation in shades depending on the composition of the alloys used. The panel surrounding the exhaust manifold was stainless steel, and thus shows a darker hue in photographs.

'In-the-field' camouflage

Concern about the conspicuousness of unpainted
aircraft led VIII Fighter Command to advise its
fighter groups in May 1944 to apply camouflage
paints to the uppersurfaces of front line fighters.
It was anticipated that following the forthcoming
cross-Channel invasion of the Continent, fighters
would be moved to airfields in liberated areas.
Strangely, the Ninth Air Force, whose fighters it
was planned would operate from the bridgehead
as soon as possible, did not issue similar advice
to its units. While no orders are recalled
specifically directing certain groups to carry out

P-51D-10-NA 44-14660 of the 364th FS/357th FG, Leiston, August 1944
Assigned to Gerald E Tyler in September 1944, 44-14660 boasted green and grey camouflage paint applied 'in-the-field' by the 357th FG at its Leiston base. Like Tyler's P-51C (43-6376 C5-J) that this aircraft replaced, the name LITTLE DUCKFOOT was painted on both sides of the engine cowling. Tyler qualified for ace status, but none of his seven victories was obtained with this aircraft.

ABOVE: Battle-damaged P-51B 42-106447 has top decking with unit applied dark green, which was common on many early 357th FG Mustangs that received 'in-the-field' camouflage. Note the unusually shaped letter L, complete with a lower lip. The same shape appeared on later Ls of the 364th FS, indicating use of the same stencil.

this work, it is a fact that while some added camouflage to virtually all their assigned aircraft, others only painted up the odd machine. Among Mustang-equipped units, the 357th FG was the prime example of the former measure, while the 355th and 361st had several with camouflage added and the 4th, 339th, 352nd and 359th FGs had none, or just the odd example.

In the 357th, many P-51Bs had only the upper decking of the fuselage painted either in British-sourced Dark Green or US Dark Olive Drab. The uppersurfaces of the wings and empennage were also painted, while the undersurfaces of the wings and fuselage remained in natural metal.

A further development was to give a camouflage coating along the lines of that applied at the factories before camouflage paint was discontinued. Uppersurfaces were sprayed Dark Green and the undersurfaces usually Sky (a blue-grey British shade) or a light grey.

The 355th FG used similar schemes to the 357th, with several P-51B/Cs in the 354th FS given dark green upper and light grey undersurfaces, while others, particularly after D-Day, simply had the uppersurfaces of the wings, tailplane and upper fuselage decking painted dark green and the remainder of the aircraft, including the fin and rudder, left unpainted. However, there were always several bare metal finish Mustangs in the other squadrons that received no unit-applied camouflage.

The 361st FG had only a limited number of aircraft with 'in-the-field' camouflage, the majority of its Mustangs remaining 'silver'. Dark green was applied to the uppersurfaces of the wings, tailplanes and upper fuselage decking, as well as around the edges of the fin and rudder. As a complete change, at least two 361st Mustangs had areas of Insignia Blue on the fuselage instead of dark green.

BELOW: Locked brakes caused the collapse of the main landing gear of this 361st FG P-51C. The black band has been removed from the fin and rudder, and in so doing part of the project number 64 has also been removed. So-called Project Numbers were applied at US modification centres or production plants to ready a required number of aircraft of a certain specification to meet a particular military requirement. On P-51Bs and Ds, they were often seen adjacent to the fuselage data panel, whereas P-51Cs carried these markings on rudders.

P-51D-5-NA 44-13926 of the 375th FS/361st FG, Bottisham, August 1944
Delivered to the 361st FG's Bottisham base in July 1944, this Mustang has been identified with Abe P Rosenberger, although several other pilots are known to have flown it. The fighter enjoyed a front line life of just under a month, for on 9 August 1944 it crashed 60 miles from Bottisham during a training flight, killing pilot Donald Dellinger – the latter had been with the group for just a matter of days. The Mustang's green camouflage on its uppersurfaces was applied 'in-the-field' (see page 16 for photographs showing both sides of this P-51D in flight).

No examples of unit-applied camouflage are known for 339th, 352nd and 359th FG Mustangs, and while the 4th FG did not engage in this practice prior to D-Day either, two of its aircraft did receive camouflage paint at a later date, but on the whim of a senior officer. The first example was Lt Col Claiborne Kinnard's P-51D-10 44-14292 QP-A, which he flew after assuming command of the Group in November 1944. This had a swirl of dark green along the top of the fuselage and a disruptive pattern of the same colour on the bare metal uppersurfaces of the wings and tailplane. The pattern was made up of narrow wavy bands angled out from the leading to trailing edges. Later in January 1945, the CO of the 334th FS, Maj Howard 'Deacon' Hively, had the uppersurfaces of his P-51D-15 44-15347 QP-J painted dark green, although the undersurfaces of the fighter remained untouched.

Unit-applied camouflage was discontinued in most squadrons in July and August 1944. Ironically, when two Eighth Air Force Mustang groups were detached to operate from continental bases in December 1944, those selected were the 352nd FG, which had not indulged in applying camouflage paints, and the 361st FG, which by that time was equipped almost entirely with 'silver' aircraft!

D-Day stripes

Officially known as the Allied Expeditionary Air Forces Special Marking, the black and white stripes that adorned most tactical aircraft involved in the cross-Channel invasion of 6 June 1944 were commonly called Invasion Stripes, or D-Day Stripes. With the anticipation that the *Luftwaffe* would respond in strength when the landings took place, there was a danger that Allied aircraft would be mistaken for the enemy in some situations. To minimise this risk it was decided to give all tactical aircraft a special distinctive marking. Application was ordered on the late afternoon of 3 June, with all aircraft to be painted up within 48 hours. When the Invasion was delayed for a day due to poor weather, all aircraft painted with the stripes were generally grounded until further notice.

The application instruction for single-engined aircraft required five alternating 18-inch wide stripes – white, black, white, black, white – around the rear fuselage and each wing. On the latter, the edge of the outer white stripe was to be six inches from the national insignia. On the fuselage the edge of the rearmost white stripe was to be 18 inches from the leading edge of the tailplane, but the stripes should not obscure the national marking.

These general instructions could not be adhered to exactly on different aircraft types, although on the P-51B/C the variation only amounted to an inch or two. On the wings, the innermost white stripe was usually placed on the type identity band, and actually made use of this if the aircraft had camouflage finish. On the fuselage, the rearmost edge of the stripes was often under 18 inches from the tailplane, but again only by an inch or two. The outer white fuselage stripes obliterated most of the individual aircraft letter and the second character of the squadron code. In some cases these were painted around, and in others reinstated. On some camouflaged aircraft where characters had been painted in white, this resulted in letters being part white and part black, or sometimes just a black outline of that part on the white stripe.

Each group had its own ideas about reinstating the unit markings, although there were many exceptions. In the 4th FG the characters were reinstated in the original colour, or painted around. As all 339th FG P-51s were in natural metal finish, the partly painted-out codes and individual letters were reinstated in black. The 352nd FG reinstated the squadron code in black on the white band, but not the individual aircraft letter. In the 328th and 487th FSs the letter

ABOVE: The Mustangs of 361st FG had their code letters quickly reinstated after D-Day stripes were applied. Yellow-nosed P-51B 42-106655 B7-<u>H</u> was the assigned aircraft of Wallace Hopkins, CO of the 374th FS. It was named *Ferocious Frankie*, as were his other personal mounts. The name was applied in red. Note that the 'long-range tank installed' cross symbol was stencilled on in black on unpainted finishes.

RIGHT: A red-nosed 336th FS P-51B with full D-Day stripes, bombed-up for a fighter-bomber mission. This photograph was taken shortly before 43-6942 VF-D was flown by assigned pilot Joe Higgens on the June 1944 shuttle mission to the USSR. The painted-out type identity band on the fin shows up clearly in this photograph.

P-51B-5-NA 43-6754 of the 487th FS/352nd FG, Bodney, 6 June 1944
The camouflaged P-51Bs received as original equipment by the 352nd FG wore a lighter, brighter shade of blue for the group's now famous nose marking. Although the personal Mustang of Ralph Hamilton from April through to September 1944, the four enemy aircraft known to have been shot down by 43-6754 were all claimed by other pilots. In September 1944, Hamilton received a P-51D, but 43-6754 remained with the 352nd FG until written-off whilst serving as a training aircraft in February 1945.

RIGHT: In the 355th FG, the squadron codes were not usually obscured when D-Day stripes were applied. P-51B 43-6523 YF-E carried 58 sortie symbols, but this tally probably included all of assigned pilot Charles Blair's missions in other aircraft too. The fighter was lost with another pilot on 19 June 1944.

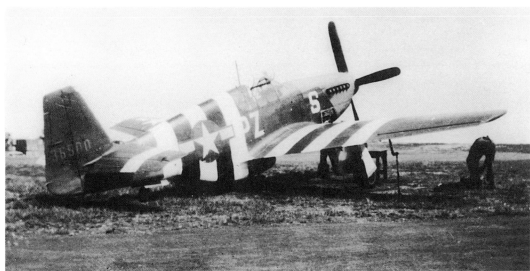

LEFT: When D-Day stripes were applied to Mustangs of the 486th FS, the covered individual aircraft letter was repainted just aft of the exhaust manifold on both sides of the nose, size and colour as standard. P-51B 43-6500 PZ-S has the early bright blue nose marking of the 352nd FG.

was painted on the tail fin instead, while the 486th FS placed it on the forward fuselage just aft of the exhaust stacks. These letters were 24 inches high – the same as those covered by the D-Day stripes. Later, the 486th FS also placed the individual letter on the fin.

The 355th FG did not paint over the squadron code or aircraft letter when applying the stripes, while the squadrons of the 357th FG generally favoured different ways to reinstate the codes. The 362nd FS tended to repaint the characters in the original colour. The 363rd FS, which had mostly camouflaged aircraft, painted the obliterated characters on the white stripe in black, thus having one letter of the code in white and the other in black. However, several aircraft of this squadron had the B6 code painted afresh forward of the D-Day stripes. The 364th FS, also having camouflaged aircraft, had one letter of the code in white and the other in black as an almost standard feature following the application of the stripes. Finally, within the 359th and 361st FGs, the code and individual letters that were originally obliterated by D-Day stripes were eventually reinstated in the appropriate colour.

Soon after the Invasion, with many Ninth Air Force fighters operating from advanced landing grounds in the Normandy beachhead area, the D-Day stripes were considered to compromise camouflage, so a general instruction was issued, effective 4 July, that the stripes were to be removed from the uppersurfaces of wings and fuselage. It took some days for all Eighth Air Force fighters to have these removed – particularly those with bare metal finish, where paint stripper had to be used. Another instruction required the underwing stripes to be removed between 25 August and 10 September. Finally, in early December, the remaining portion of the Invasion marking on the underside of the fuselage was ordered to be deleted by the last day of the year. In practice, the underfuselage stripes were still to be seen on some aircraft several weeks into 1945.

LEFT: Battle-damaged P-51B 42-106809 CV-H sports a green nose and full D-Day stripes. This photograph was taken on, or shortly after, 6 June 1944, and before code letters had been reinstated. CV-H was later named *Little Liquidator* and eventually relegated for use in training (coded CV-O), only to be lost in the North Sea on 7 February 1945.

RIGHT: A trio of 376th FS Mustangs at Bottisham with full D-Day stripes. The centre aircraft, named *Elizabeth*, was notable for the shark's mouth design on its nose, reminiscent of the decoration often seen on Curtiss P-40s in North Africa and China. At least three 361st FG aircraft boasted this decoration.

RIGHT: This flight of 374th FS Mustangs, photographed in late July 1944, exhibit a variety of markings. The two P-51Bs (42-106942 B7-H and 42-106839 B7-E) have unit-applied camouflage to the rear fuselage decking and the upper wing surfaces to a point just short of the national insignia. Type identity bands have been removed from all four and D-Day stripes are only retained on the wing and fuselage undersides. The two P-51Ds (44-13357 B7-R and 44-13857 B7-O) both have blue wing tips, which were applied as a flight colour. The former also has a blue trim tab. B7-R, named *TIKA IV* and boasting six victory symbols, was the aircraft assigned to Vernon Richards. P-51B 42-106839 B7-E *BALD EAGLE III* presumably belongs to the same flight, but has its wing tips and trim tab striped blue and yellow. The area between the anti-glare panel and the engine exhaust manifold was also decorated with yellow and blue striping.

LEFT: Maj Hopkins' replacement for the P-51B illustrated on page 12 was also named *Ferocious Frankie*. The name was painted in black and the victory markings were stencilled onto a red band. The aircraft was also coded B7-H.

BELOW: Another 374th FS P-51D with a yellow trim tab outlined with black. Not all aircraft assigned to this squadron received the flight colour, as this was more a groundcrew fancy than an official requirement. *DUCHESS of MANHATTAN* was usually flown by Henry Lederer.

LEFT: P-51B 42-106944 E9-A *Flying Jeanie III* of the 376th FS/361st FG, clutching two silver 110 US gallon drop tanks, shows that its worn underwing D-Day stripes have been outlined to make them more visible. The aircraft was wrecked four weeks after this photograph was taken when it was shot down by flak over Germany on 13 September 1944.

BELOW: 375th FS P-51D 44-13568 E2-A *Sky Bouncer* has similar markings to those worn by fellow 361st FG Mustang *Flying Jeanie III*, including the black type identity bands on the tailplane.

ABOVE AND RIGHT: A good example of unit-applied camouflage is that seen on P-51D 44-13926 E2-S, photographed in July 1944 when D-Day stripes had been removed from the uppersurfaces of Allied fighters. The paint is believed to have been British-sourced Dark Green, which was similar in shade to Dark Olive Drab. Undersurfaces and lower areas of the fuselage were left as bare metal. It is believed that only around a score of 361st FG Mustangs received 'in-the-field' camouflage. The pilot of E2-S, when these photographs were taken, was Urban Drew, who later achieved ace status.

P-51B-10-NA 42-106702 of the 368th FS/359th FG, East Wretham, July 1944
One of the complement of P-51Bs used to re-equip the 359th FG in May 1944, CV-X was
first assigned to Robert V Beaupre and then John B Hunter. This aircraft was lost during a
dive-bombing attack on the marshalling yard at Bishwiller, in France, on 10 August 1944,
its pilot, Lester Hovden, being killed when he made a sharp 45-degree turn to line up on his
target and overstressed the Mustang's bomb-laden airframe. Both wings folded up and then
separated from the fuselage, the wingless fighter hitting the ground and exploding
moments later. Bright, grass green paint was used for the group marking on the first 359th
Mustangs, but later aircraft in metal finish featured darker shades.

ABOVE AND ABOVE RIGHT: Russell McNally's first
P-51B was 43-6815 YF-O, which was apparently
denuded of camouflage paint in the summer of
1944. On the right side of the nose it carried a
comical reference to the pilot, *Bo-Mc*. On the left
side the aircraft's given name was *MORPHINE SUE*,
together with a girlie motif. The fighter retains the
D-Day stripes under the wings and rear fuselage.
Its spinner and nose band were white, which was
the 355th FG's official recognition colours.

LEFT: A collision
caused much damage
to the right wing of
P-51B *Jackie II*
(43-24796 6N-O). Of
interest is the winged
B on the fin, indicating
a B Flight aircraft of
the 505th FS.

Conversion of the P-38 groups

A month after D-Day, VIII Fighter Command resumed the programme of converting its groups to Mustangs, the four P-38 Lightning groups being next in line. The 20th and 55th FGs began training on Mustangs at around about the same time, and they duly became operational on the new fighter within a matter of days of each other – the 55th first on 19 July and the 20th the very next day.

The latter group had used yellow as its group identification colour while flying P-38s, but this was already the hallmark of 361st FG Mustangs. Therefore, although the 20th FG used the same codes as carried by its Lightnings – KI for the 55th FS, LC for the 77th and MC for the 79th, as well as the same tail shapes (a triangle, circle and square for the 55th, 77th and 79th respectively) – a new nose marking had to be devised. Initially, this simply entailed painting part of the type identity nose marking white (the front 12 inches of the spinner and a five-inch wide band backing the black nose band). There was some variation in the width of the nose bands, but this remained the group marking until November 1944, when a series of alternating black and white stripes were added, extending back towards the cockpit to a point above the wing leading edge.

LEFT: White does not always show up clearly in monochrome photographs, but the 20th FG's black and white design is plain to see on this pair of 79th FS P-51Ds, hugging 108 US gallon 'paper' drop tanks. The 20th continued to use the geometric shapes on the vertical tail that had previously been introduced to make it easier to tell the squadron identity of its P-38s. The individual plane-in-squadron letter was painted on this black shape, as well as in the standard position for P-51s – the rear fuselage. 44-13876 MC-M was assigned to Robert Meyer and 44-13620 MC-H to Arthur Heiden.

P-51D-5-NA 44-14337 of the 77th FS/20th FG, Kings Cliffe, August 1944
This aircraft was chosen by Col Harold J Rau as his personal mount upon returning from leave in the USA, and prior to taking command of the 20th FG in late August 1944. As with the previous P-38 Lightnings that he had flown during his command of this group between March and June 1944, Rau named the P-51 *"GENTLE ANNIE"* and had the codes MC-R applied to its flanks. When he left the group in December 1944, the aircraft was taken over by Darrell Beschen and renamed *Wildarcliff III/Bridget's Bunion*.

In addition to carrying individual aircraft letters on the rear fuselage in the approved size for P-51s, 20th FG aircraft also had the letter repeated on the black geometric shape carried on the vertical tail surfaces. Painted in white, this letter was the same size – 24 inches high – as that on the fuselage.

The 55th FG, setting out to apply similar style markings to its Mustang as carried by its Lightnings, had the fin and rudder sprayed Dark Green and the squadron geometric shape painted thereon in white. These were a triangle, circle (disc) and square for the 38th, 338th and 343rd FSs respectively. Most Mustangs also had the uppersurface of the tailplane and about

LEFT: Taxiing out for a mission, P-51s of the 79th FS pass the Kings Cliffe control tower. Dark green unit-applied camouflage on the uppersurfaces was also carried up the fin and rudder, leaving an unpainted area around the geometric shape. Tail numbers were usually removed on most aircraft. MC-F was P-51D 44-13751 *Wanda's Worry*, flown by Robert Campbell.

RIGHT: When the 55th FG commenced its conversion to Mustangs in late June 1944, the geometric shapes previously used used on the twin tails of its P-38s were also painted on the newly arrived P-51s for squadron identification purposes. The uppersurfaces of the tail were painted dark green and the squadron marking applied in white, as on this P-51D (44-13368) of the 338th FS, which soon came to grief. The white nose may possibly have been a base colour for the yellow and white checkerboard originally allotted to the 55th as a group marking on P-38s, but never used.

BELOW: A green and yellow checkerboard nose band was eventually adopted as the group marking and squadron code letters painted on in the standard locations. Stencil breaks were very evident on the first 55th Mustangs to receive codes, P-51D 44-14751 being amongst the early aircraft assigned to the unit.

ABOVE: The 338th FS chose to back the yellow and green checkerboard with a six-inch band of dark green, as seen on P-51C 43-25037 CL-L. The name *JESIE-MAY* was painted in yellow.

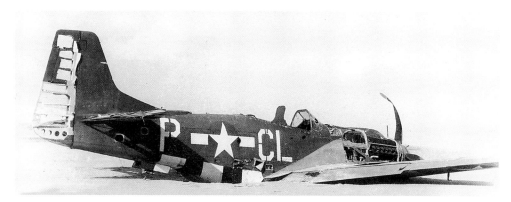

LEFT: A camouflage paint scheme devised by an artist at VIII Fighter Command HQ was adopted by the 55th FG and applied to several of its Mustangs during August and September 1944. It consisted of painting the upper-surfaces of the tail and the rear fuselage dark green, with this paintwork terminating at the wing trailing edge, but being carried forward in a diagonal sweep up the fuselage to meet the anti-dazzle panel forward of the windshield. The tail number was generally not reinstated, as on P-51D 44-13954, assigned to John McGinn. It was being flown by Samuel Gevorkian when it ran out of fuel and crash-landed at Cape Ferrat, in France, on 26 August 1944.

24 inches of the fuselage decking just forward of the fin also painted with camouflage green. Unlike the 20th FG, the 55th FG did not have individual aircraft letters painted on the geometric shape. Finally, squadron codes remained as they were for the P-38 – CG, CL and CY for the 38th, 338th and 343rd FSs respectively.

In March 1944 the 55th had been assigned yellow and white checkerboards as a group marking, but this was never applied presumably because of the work involved in physically painting it onto the P-38, and the group's scheduled conversion to the Mustang. All the P-51Ds sent to the 55th at Wormingford, in Essex, were bare metal finish, and had black type identity markings. Some of these had their noses painted white, but whether this was preparatory to receiving yellow and white checkerboards is not known. In any case, these early markings on the group's Mustangs were short-lived for the tail shapes were painted out and green and yellow checkerboards adopted as the 55th's identity, in line with other units controlled by the 66th Fighter Wing.

The green used by the 55th was apparently the same camouflage dark green as applied to the P-51s' tails. In fact, it was so dark that from only a hundred yards in bright conditions the checkerboard appeared as black and yellow, rather than green and yellow. The spinner was divided into three encircling bands of yellow, green and yellow.

In mid-July 1944, an artist at VIII Fighter Command HQ devised a paint scheme for 55th FG Mustangs, and part of this was adopted but probably not applied to more than a score of the Group's aircraft. It consisted of spraying the uppersurface of the empennage and rear fuselage camouflage green. The scheme was extended forward to the trailing edge of the wing, then swept up to merge with the anti-dazzle panel in front of the cockpit. A six-inch wide red band edged the dark green. On the tail, type identity bands were reinstated in white.

P-51D-10-NA 44-14561 of the 343rd FS/55th FG, Wormingford, September 1944
This aircraft featured the pseudo-camouflage paint scheme that was applied to a handful of the 55th FG's aircraft in the late summer of 1944. Assigned to ground-strafing ace (and 121-mission veteran) Frank Birtciel, 44-14561 was named for his future wife. The aircraft was notified as salvaged on 3 October 1944, Birtciel replacing it with P-51D 44-13350 CY-A, which he also named *MISS VELMA*.

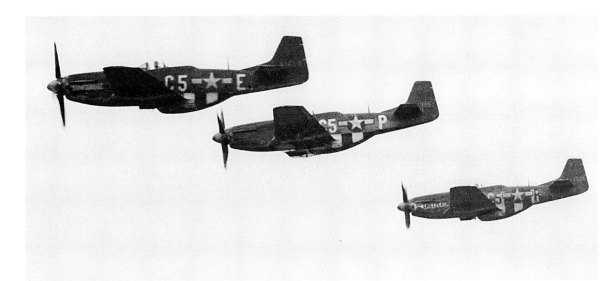

LEFT: Like the P-51Ds of the 363rd FS, the 364th's mostly had complete suits of camouflage – dark green upper and light grey undersurfaces. In this flight are 44-14507 C5-E *TANGERINE* 44-13981 C5-P and 44-13546 C5-R *The Shillelagh*.

ABOVE, ABOVE RIGHT AND RIGHT: 'In-the-field' camouflage on 362nd FS Mustangs was usually confined to the uppersurfaces of the wing and tailplane, the fin and rudder and the top decking of the fuselage. G4-G 44-13719 was distinctive in having a six-inch wide band of dark green backing the group red and yellow checkered nose marking. The significance of this band has not been ascertained, but presumably was a pilot or groundcrew fancy – note also the discharge of oil from a breather outlet below the exhaust stubs. Before being lost on 30 December 1944, this aircraft is reported to have gained the name *Pitter Pat*. *Sweet Helen II* (44-13558 G4-B) was the assigned aircraft of Harvey Mace, while the regular pilot of G4-U 44-13334 *WEE WILLY II* was Calvert Williams, and the far P-51D, 44-13596 G4-S *Betsy*, was Harry Ankeny's mount. All these names were painted on in red.

The 364th FG was the next to shed its P-38 Lightnings for P-51s, becoming operational on the type in late July 1944. As with the previous two ex-Lightning groups, the 364th used the same geometric shapes on the fins and rudders of its P-51s for squadron identification – the 383rd, 384th and 385th FSs were identified by a circle, square and triangle, respectively. Like the 20th FG, the 364th had individual letters applied to its fighters in white over the tail marking, but unlike the former, no individual aircraft letter was carried on the fuselage. Only the squadron codes were painted on the fuselage, and always aft of the national insignia. These were N2 for the 383rd FS, 5Y for the 384th and 5E for the 385th.

ABOVE AND BELOW: Roy Osborn commanded the 364th FG when it converted from P-38s to P-51s. His personal Mustang was serviced by the 383rd FS and coded N2-O, the O standing for Osborn. The name *Billy's Boy* was painted in blue.

ABOVE: A white spinner and blue and white nose band identified 364th FG Mustangs. The application of the blue and white segments was generally uniform, with a blue segment just below the exhaust manifold on both sides of the aircraft. *Coffin Wit' Wings*, alias 44-14322 5E-O, exhibits a common feature on P-51s during the last few months of hostilities – the marking of individual engine panels with the last three or four digits of the serial number. This number was applied to ensure that when aircraft were parked in close proximity undergoing maintenance, the engine panels would not get mixed up. Although a mass-produced aircraft, there was often a slight variation in the assembly of the engine compartment framing and panels.

P-51D-20-NA 44-63263 of the 384th FS/364th FG, Honington, February 1945
This aircraft was assigned to 7.5-kill ace John H Lowell, who served both as CO of the 384th FS and then Deputy CO of the 364th FG. It replaced his previous P-51D (44-14992 5Y-L *Penny 3*), which was shot down by flak near Limburg, in Germany, whilst being flown by Capt Jack V Johnson on 12 December 1944, the pilot being killed. Carrying the name *Penny 4* on its port side, 44-63263 proved unlucky in aerial combat, for 157-mission veteran Lowell failed to claim a single aerial kill with it. For some unexplained reason, the fighter's replacement rudder was adorned only with the 384th's L-Square marking and not its complete serial.

Whereas the 20th FG's geometric devices on the tail were a fairly standard 30 inches at the widest or highest point, those on 364th FG aircraft varied considerably. For example, on the tails of 383rd FS P-51s, the disc was 40 inches in diameter, with the letter thereon being about 30 inches high. The 384th's square was much smaller with only 24-inch sides, whilst the letter was about 18 inches high. The 385th's triangle was 36 inches high with a 28-inch base, and the letters thereon were approximately 24 inches high. However, smaller circles and triangles were to be seen. As with the 20th FG, the 364th's geometric shapes mostly obscured tail numbers, although in some cases these were repainted.

Like the 20th FG, the 364th had to find new group markings, as white, used on its P-38s, was the identification colour for 355th FG Mustangs. The spinner and nose band were painted

BELOW AND RIGHT: The 383rd FS's black disc on its Mustangs' tails was approximately 40 inches in diameter on the first P-51Ds received, and the letter thereon 30 inches high. Most of the tail number was obscured and not repainted. These two views of 44-13707 N2-E show the type identity markings on the wings and tailplane and the remnants of D-Day stripes, which were only retained on the underside of the fuselage after August 1944. Assigned to John Hunter, the aircraft was listed as missing with another pilot on 26 November 1944. By then it carried the name *Lady Dorothy IV* on the left side of the nose.

ABOVE: The triangle on 385th FS Mustangs was usually clear of the tail number. This P-51D (44-13994 5E-N) shows signs of paint having been removed from its nose section, the fighter having previously served with the 359th FG's 370th FS as CS-B. It was shot down by an Me 262 on 22 February 1945.

LEFT: The battle-damaged tail of Donald Bloodgood's P-51D 44-14254 5E-G reveals that the letter G was painted in red, and that the fin fillet and tail trim tabs are red with dark blue stripes. At least three other aircraft in this squadron are known to have had similar markings, but whether they served a purpose or were just decorations has not been ascertained by the author.

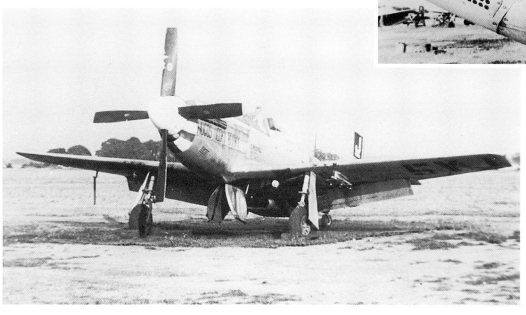

LEFT AND ABOVE: P-51D 44-13993 5Y-J *HUGO'S NOOKY BOOKY* advertised that this was Hugo Lohr's aircraft. The colour of the inscription is believed to have been blue.

LEFT AND BELOW:
Just Plain L, another 384th FS aircraft, also acknowledged the pilot, Lee LeForge. For some reason this P-51D had lost most of its tail number, although 413 is just discernible.

ABOVE: Getting a barred letter into the 24-inch square used by the 384th FS did not leave much room. Carrying a barred V, P-51D 44-14210 was the second V-Victor in the unit.

RIGHT: In the 383rd FS barred letters were presented in the form of two small blocks on each side of the letter, as with 43-25066 N2-Y. Placing the squadron code forward of the national insignia was uncommon on 364th FG Mustangs.

white, but medium blue stripes, six inches wide, were painted thereon with six to eight inches separation. Only an odd example of 'in-the-field' camouflage was seen on 364th FG Mustangs at Honington, in Suffolk, and these aircraft may have been inherited from another group.

A shortage of P-51Ds delayed the conversion of the 479th FG from the P-38 until September 1944. The group's form of identification with the Lightning was simply no spinner or backing colour band, and this was also the case with its Mustangs. Being devoid of camouflage paint, they were seen with bare metal spinners and engine cowlings. The same squadron code letters used on P-38s were also carried on the P-51s, these being L2 for the 434th FS, J2 for the 435th and 9B for the 436th.

In August the 479th FG had adopted coloured rudders for extra squadron identification in place of geometric shapes, and these coloured rudders were also used on the Mustangs. The 434th used red and the 435th yellow, but whereas the 436th had previously been identified as the squadron of the Group without a rudder colour when equipped with P-38s, it started to use a black and white checkerboard on its Mustangs. The contrasting squares were 12 inches square, but it is doubtful that all the Squadron's aircraft were so painted before this design was abandoned in favour of all-black rudders.

In painting the rudders, part of the tail number was obscured, and on the majority of the Group's Mustangs, the remainder of the number on the fin was removed. On a few, the number

ABOVE LEFT AND ABOVE: Many 4th FG P-51Ds had no flamboyant personal markings during the summer of 1944, and black type identity bands on the vertical tail surfaces were retained. Typical are 44-13306 QP-F and 44-13961 VF-L, the first being written off in an accident and the second being listed as missing in action on 8 November 1944.

P-51D-10-NA 44-14354 of the 435th FS/479th FG, Wattisham, January 1945
Amongst the first batch of P-51Ds received by the 435th FS as replacements for its P-38Js in late September 1944, this aircraft was assigned to Phillip D Gossard until he returned to the USA, tour-expired, in December 1944. In common with most 479th FG Mustangs, its serial number was removed at the same time as the black type identity markings, and the squadron colours were applied to the rudder. It is believed that the veteran fighter had its tail number reinstated towards the end of hostilities.

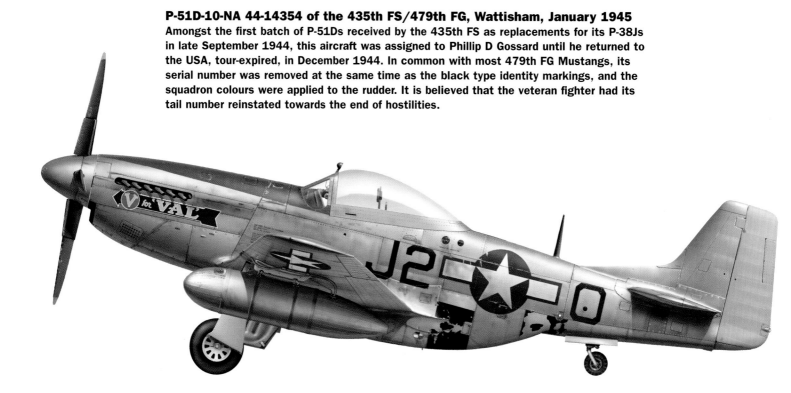

was reinstated in black or white as appropriate. Black type identity bands were also removed from 479th P-51s. There were, as usual with aircraft markings, exceptions to the rule.

Further P-47 group conversions

Although the supply of new P-51s was limited during the autumn of 1944, conversion of the remaining P-47-equipped groups got underway in September 1944, with the 353rd FG at Raydon, in Suffolk, performing its first mission with the type on 2 October. The Group's eye-catching yellow and black group marking was also applied to its new Mustangs, spinners being divided into four equal width, encircling bands of black, yellow, black, yellow, while the backing cowling band consisted of six-inch black and yellow checkers. Unlike the other groups assigned to the 66th Fighter Wing, the 353rd FG's identity bands were made up of three instead of two rows of checkers. Squadron codes applied to the Mustangs were the same as had been worn by the now discarded P-47s, namely LH for the 350th FS, YJ for 351st and SX for 352nd.

RIGHT AND BELOW: One of the first combat Mustangs received by the 353rd FG at Raydon went to 352nd FS CO William Bailey – seen here with his groundcrew and his dog. As with his other fighters, this P-51D (44-14303) was coded SX-B, and like many other Mustangs in the group, it was decorated with small motifs on circular backgrounds. The Group's yellow and black checkerboard ran to three rows of six-inch squares, and the spinner was divided into approximately seven-inch bands of yellow and black, plus a black tip. This aircraft was lost with another pilot on 3 February 1945. The lower photograph shows William Bailey's replacement P-51D, 44-63834 *Double Trouble Too*.

RIGHT: One of the first combat P-51Ds of the 356th FG, 44-15101 QI-I was eventually assigned to Edward Faison. Photographed in flight soon after its arrival with the group, the Mustang had yet to receive the 356th's new colours in place of the black type identity markings on the nose.

In November the 356th FG at Martlesham Heath, in Suffolk, became the next fighter group to switch to Mustangs. Its P-47s had previously been recognised by not having any coloured nose markings, but as 479th FG P-51s were identified by this means, a new group marking had to be found. The 356th chose blue and red for its new group marking, the P-51's spinner being encircled with bands in these colours. The rear portion, nine inches wide, was applied in blue, followed by six two-inch wide alternating bands of red and blue, with a red tip. The red cowling band backing the spinner was extended up and back just under the exhaust manifold and then up and back to the cockpit, the anti-glare panel being incorporated in this red cover.

P-51D-10-NA 44-14610 of the 351st FS/353rd FG, Raydon, January 1945
One of the first P-51Ds obtained by the 351st FS at Raydon in November 1944, 44-14610 was assigned to Capt Harold Chase. 2Lt John G 'Billy' Lancaster was flying it when he was forced to make a crash-landing in bad weather on 15 February 1945 upon returning from a bomber escort mission to Germany. Flying into thick cloud over the continent, which caused his squadron to split up, Lancaster asked for a homing whilst over the Thames Estuary. Brought in over land, his engine cut through fuel starvation before he could be brought down safely, and Lancaster was left with little option but to crash-land at Church Farm, near Stockbury, Kent. Suffering significant damage in the incident, 44-14610 was nevertheless initially considered worthy of repair, for it was not declared salvaged until after VE-Day. Officially, the cause of the accident was blamed on poor weather and poor flying technique on 2Lt Lancaster's part, as it was discovered that he did not switch from his empty right fuel tank to a new fuel tank in time to prevent the engine quitting.

RIGHT: The 368th FS was unusual in that the rudder trim tabs of its Mustangs were painted green during the summer of 1944 as an additional aid to squadron recognition. P-51D 44-13669 CV-I also had its nickname – *Pegelin* – applied in green, as was the four-leaf clover. Assigned to Glenn Bach, it went missing with another pilot on 5 October 1944. The camouflaged P-51B (CV-P) was 43-12478, which had been one of the first Mustangs assigned to the 354th FG in 1943. It eventually found its way to the 359th after major repairs, and survived operations to be converted into a two-seat trainer, coded CV-P.

ABOVE AND ABOVE RIGHT: A darker green for the nose marking came into use on metal finish P-51Ds of the 359th FG during the summer of 1944. CS-K 44-13966 was devoid of personal insignia, whereas many Mustangs of the group had very flamboyant decor. Originally assigned to John B Murphy, this aircraft was later passed to Robert York, who became an ace. A good example of flashy markings was Claude Crenshaw's *HEAT WAVE*, alias 44-15016 IV-I, with this name spread out along the side of the engine compartment in flaming red letters.

LEFT: When the 359th FG began using a darker green for the group nose marking, its contrast with olive drab was not so marked, as clearly shown with this P-51B inherited from another unit. *HOT PANTS* (red letters with incomplete white outlines) was 43-6461 CS-Q, which Wilson Baker had to land in Sweden on 4 August 1944, where this photograph was taken. It was one of three 359th FG machines that made emergency recoveries in the neutral Scandinavian country on this day due to fuel shortages.

Superimposed on the red base were longitudinal rows of blue diamonds, approximately eight inches long by four inches high. The number and placement of the diamonds varied from aircraft to aircraft. Mostly, there was a single chain of diamonds encircling the cowling directly aft of the spinner, and five rows of diamonds over the top of the cowling from above one manifold to the other. Squadron codes were as carried on the P-47s – OC, PI and QI for the 359th, 360th and 361st FSs respectively.

The last of the 14 Eighth Air Force fighter groups to be equipped with the Mustang was the 78th FG at Duxford, in Cambridgeshire. Conversion started in December 1944, and the Group's last Thunderbolt operation was flown the following January. The black and white checkerboard synonymous with the 78th's P-47s was perpetuated as the group recognition marking, initially with eight-inch squares, six per horizontal line on the front of the engine cowling. These were stylised with a rear line sweep down and forward from the anti-glare panel, which eliminated the number of squares per lower line to five.

However, very few aircraft received this form of nose marking before it was replaced by one incorporating eight six-inch squares per horizontal line, as with the 353rd FG's checkerboard. This arrangement was further embellished by a two-inch wide red border backing the rear of the checkerboard and swept back low down to the wing root. Further checkers were added with the sweep back, and there were usually 12 squares per longitudinal row between the spinner and wing root.

Instead of the appropriate colour bands which other 66th Fighter Wing group Mustangs wore on their spinners, the 78th painted the spinner half white and half black along a longitudinal axis. When the spinner turned, it produced a pronounced flickering effect, although this appeared to the eye as a far slower rotation than was actually the case. Code letters carried were identical to those used on the group's P-47s – MX for the 82nd FS, HL for the 83rd and WZ for the 84th, all painted in black in the standard size.

BELOW: Raymond Smith's 44-63712 WZ-B *FLY'N TIME BOMB* carried 28 locomotive symbols for his ground-strafing exploits shooting up rail traffic. In addition, there were eight swastika symbols on the canopy frame for the destruction of one enemy aircraft in the air and seven on the ground. Smith flew two tours with the 84th FS. This P-51D was lost at the hands of another pilot on 21 April 1945.

ABOVE: The first black and white checkerboard devised for 78th FG Mustangs was composed of 12-inch squares, but this was quickly replaced by a more extensive six-inch scheme. The posed antics in the photograph were to show pilots' supposed disapproval of having to forsake P-47s for P-51s.

P-51D-20-NA 44-63620 of the 83rd FS/78th FG, Duxford, April 1945

This aircraft was assigned to John A Kirk III when the group transitioned from P-47Ds to P-51Ds in December 1944, the fighter boasting ten victory symbols for its pilot's four aerial claims and six strafing kills (not all obtained in this aircraft) just forward of the cockpit. 44-63620 was written off in a crash-landing at Duxford in May 1945. The red outline to the group checkerboard was common to all 78th FG Mustangs by the spring of 1945. Black and white wing tips were a popular addition, but not command authorised.

P-51D-5-NT 44-11193 of the 350th FS/353rd FG, Raydon, April 1945
This Mustang was delivered to the 350th FS in November 1944 and first assigned to
Edward H Duke, who named it *My Frans*. Duke was posted Missing in Action (he was initially
captured and then escaped 11 days later, returning to Raydon on 12 April) in Mustang
44-14974 LH-Z over Germany on 17 March 1945, and George W Robison took over 44-11193
and renamed it *Marilyn II*. The fighter's final pilot in the ETO was Howard H Hakonen, who
changed the aircraft's name to *Beautiful Dope*.

Rudder colours

In October 1944 the Eighth Air Force adopted coloured
rudders as a means of additional squadron
identification, having seen that they had proved a
useful aid within the 56th and 479th FGs. These
colours, given respectively for the squadrons of a
group, were as follows: 4th FG, red, white and blue for
its 334th, 335th and 336th FS; 55th FG, no colour,
green and yellow for the 38th, 338th and 343rd FSs;
339th FG, red, dark green and no colour for its 503rd,
504th and 505th FSs; 352nd FG, red, yellow and blue
for its 328th, 486th and 487th FSs; 353rd FG, yellow,
no colour and black for its 350th, 351st and 352nd

FSs; 355th FG, red, blue and yellow for its 354th, 357th and 358th FSs; 356th FG, yellow, red
and blue for its 359th, 360th and 361st FSs; 357th FG, no colour, red and yellow for the 362nd,
363rd and 364th FSs; 359th FG, yellow, red and blue for its 368th, 369th and 370th FSs; and
the 361st FG, red, blue and yellow for the 374th, 375th and 376th FSs.

The 20th and 364th FGs retained their geometric shapes as additional squadron markings
on Mustang tails.

While in all units the red and yellow shades used were similar, the blue used by the 487th FS
was a dark shade as used in the group nose colour. Other units with blue tails used lighter shades.

Development of unit identity markings

In several units markings were changed as the weeks passed, some occasioned by a need for
better recognition, while others were the result of fancy. The 4th FG was fairly consistent with
its markings until December 1944, when an additional 12 inches was added to the red nose
band, reputedly to distinguish the group's aircraft from those of Ninth Air Force P-51 squadrons
that also had red noses. This development was short-lived in that the following month the red
paintwork was extended back and down in a stylised sweep. Around the same time the 334th

ABOVE: The
introduction of
coloured rudders as a
further means of
squadron identification
also brought an
extension of the red
nose band on 4th FG
Mustangs, this being
increased to
approximately 24
inches back to the
third exhaust outlet.
P-51D 44-14292 had
originally been
Claiborne Kinnard's
QP-A, but when the
group CO left, it was
re-coded QP-Q.
The light line aft of
the red was due to
masking tape.

RIGHT: The extended red nose band was soon extended further with a sweep down and back to a point adjacent to the wing root. *The Count*, with a character from a popular service journal cartoon, was P-51D 44-72155 QP-W, assigned to Ralph Buchanan.

FS outlined its code letters on the fuselage with red, although this practice had been seen on a few Mustangs during the previous six months. The 336th FS also depth-edged the code letters on most of its aircraft with red paint during the final months of the war. Finally, some of the group's aircraft had the lower canopy frame painted in the squadron colour, although this appears to have been at the whim of the assigned pilot or crew chief.

The 20th FG also extended its nose markings in November 1944, when alternate black and white bars were added along the sides of the cowling to a point above the leading edge of the wing. The 12-inch wide black type identity band was retained, followed by seven white and eight black bars, each six inches wide. A black border line of the same width extended back under the bars, curving up from low down on the leading black bar. There was no black band bordering the anti-glare panel, which remained in factory Olive Drab. Several 20th FG P-51s appeared with only the black bars on the cowling minus the white, probably in the cause of expediency. Some so painted are known to have had the white added at a later date.

As mentioned earlier in this book, some 20 55th FG P-51Ds received quasi-camouflage on the rear fuselage and upper tail surfaces. A red band was painted as the demarcation between the dark green and the natural metal finish. Painting Mustangs in this way was soon discontinued, but the red band was then adopted – this time two inches wide – as a border to the anti-glare panel, being continued rearwards below and right around the cockpit canopy. This became a feature of all the group's P-51s from March 1945.

P-51D-15-NA 44-15326 of the 334th FS/4th FG, Debden, December 1944
A replacement for strafing ace Gerald E Montgomery's P-51D 44-14119 *Sizzlin' Liz*, which was shot down by a Bf 109 whilst being flown by Lt Carmen Delnero (who was killed) on 21 November 1944, this aircraft sports the extended group nose marking. 44-15326 was flown by Montgomery until March 1945, when it was replaced by P-51D 44-72382, which he also named *Sizzlin' Liz*.

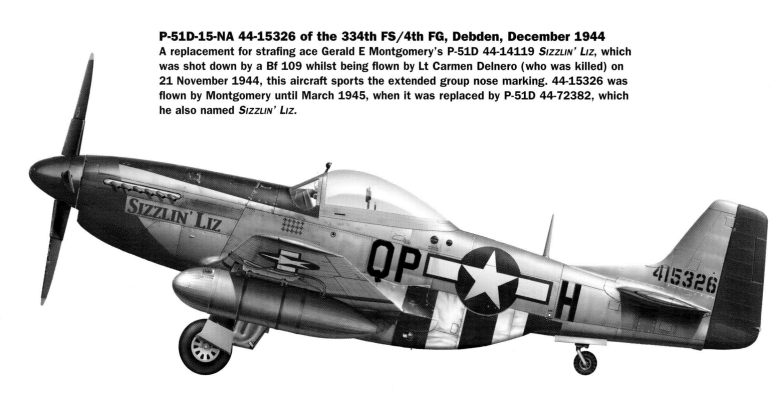

LEFT AND BELOW: Unlucky D. P-51D 44-15054 VF-D was photographed in November 1944, soon after joining the 336th FS at Debden. The rudder had been painted sky blue but the red nose band had yet to be extended. This Mustang was lost with its assigned pilot, Don Emerson, on Christmas Day 1944. Replacement P-51D 44-63233 had a similar shaped letter D and was named *Inky's Dinky* for assigned pilot George 'Ink' Davis. This Mustang was lost with another pilot on 11 February 1945.

BELOW: The 4th FG had a distinctive way of applying the bars that indicated that the wearer was the second aircraft in the unit to bear such an identifying letter. For example, P-51D WD-M– had the bar placed after the letter rather than below, as was common in most Eighth Air Force units.

LEFT AND ABOVE: Col Everett Stewart's immaculate P-51D *Sunny VIII* shows the contrast between the sky blue used for the rudder colour and the dark blue of the national insignia. The same shade applied to the rudder was also used to repaint the anti-glare panel and the canopy frame. This aircraft was wrecked in an accident in May 1945. Stewart's next VF-S (P-51D 44-72210) was specially converted at Debden into a two-seater, complete with a two-piece sliding canopy.

RIGHT: The extended nose marking of the 20th FG was certainly distinctive, with its alternating bars of black and white. Although the painting of nicknames over the group marking was frowned upon, *Janey Girl II from Texas* (in yellow) was one of several in this squadron that was so embellished. The Y-in-a-square device covered most of the tail number (472383) on this 79th FS aircraft assigned to Walter Yarborough.

BELOW: Usually aircraft names were painted below the group nose marking, as shown here on Merle Gilbertson's *Sad Sack* (44-14822 LC-A), seen here dispensing auxiliary canister smoke. The contrast between the white bars of the group marking and the bare metal finish of the aircraft shows up clearly in this photograph.

BELOW: A 343rd FS P-51K is seen undergoing maintenance in the open during the hard winter weather of 1944-45. Like a number of other 55th FG P-51s at this time, it has a red mustang on its rudder. The light band backing the nose checkers is believed to have been caused by masking tape applied when the checkerboard was painted onto the fighter.

ABOVE: The black disc on the tail of 77th FS Mustangs was usually 28 to 30 inches in diameter, and did not obscure the tail number. P-51D 44-14823 LC-F *Miss Miami* was assigned to Reps Jones.

THIS PAGE: As seen on the 55th FG P-51D on page 34, a mustang motif was applied to several 343rd FS aircraft during the winter of 1944-45. The same stencil was used in each case, but the colour and location varied. It was painted in black on the yellow rudder of Richard Ozinga's CY-M *Miss Marilyn II*, which had the dark green uniform with red band featured on some of the first 55th FG Mustangs. On Robert Buttke's *Beautiful Lavenia* CY-F, the motif was red on the rudder. The tail number was obliterated on both of these aircraft. Finally, Vincent Gordon's CY-P *Lady Val* had the mustang positioned on the fin in red, and a red band taken along the anti-glare panel and around the cockpit canopy. Tail number 414348 was painted out on the rudder.

THIS PAGE AND OPPOSITE: Variations of 343rd FS markings. P-51D 44-14985 CY-G *The Millie G*, assigned to Edward Giller, had the green uppersurface scheme but retained the black identity bands under the wings. Victor Krambo's *LUCKY WABBIT II* CY-U had its entire tail number (415406) removed. However, Patrick Moore's *Lil Jan* CY-Y retained its tail number (414235), despite the yellow rudder. This aircraft was lost on 16 April 1945. CY-K lost the 'last three' on the left side of the rudder, but retained part of the type identity stripe on the fin. Buttke's second *Beautiful Lovenia* (44-15025 CY-F) had similar treatment – the five victories adorning the fighter were all obtained by the pilot on his first tour flying P-38s. Finally, Edward Giller's last *The Millie G* (44-63204 CY-G), which was written off in this accident on 14 September 1945, had the full tail number. Three of the aircraft in this series of photographs have wider code letters than on the other aircraft of the squadron.

Soon after rudder colours were introduced, the 55th FG's 338th FS started backing the green and yellow nose checkerboard band with a six-inch wide green band in the same dark shade as used in the checkerboard, and this became a feature on all squadron aircraft. A few 343rd FS P-51s also had their rudders embellished with a red rampant mustang motif during the autumn and winter of 1944, this design also appearing on the fin of another squadron aircraft in black. In early March 1945 the 38th FS, which was formerly identified by having no special rudder colour, started to paint them red.

As the last group to convert to P-51s, the 78th FG had no major markings changes during the four months that it flew the type on operations. One embellishment that appeared on some commanders' assigned aircraft were six-inch alternating black and white bars on the wing tips. Post-war, group CO Col John Landers also had a black and white checkerboard rudder on his personal Mustang.

ABOVE: The 338th FS continued to add a six-inch green band backing the nose checkerboard on all of its aircraft. On John McGinn's 44-72296 CL-P, the tail number was left on an unpainted strip. Towards the end of the war all tail numbers were reinstated. Most of McGinn's Mustangs were christened *Da'Quake* in reference to McGinn's nickname 'Earthquake'.

RIGHT: On other 338th FS Mustangs the tail number was repainted in yellow on the green rudder, and this eventually became standard. *LITTLE TRIXIE* CL-G has the red band along the anti-dazzle panel and round the canopy. This fighter was assigned to Carroll Henry.

LEFT: P-51D 44-14598 CL-K, originally assigned to Richard Herbst, did not have the tail number replaced on the green rudder. Later named *Lady Lorene*, it was lost with another pilot on 18 March 1945.

LEFT: Ace Joe Thury flew a number of Mustangs, and he used this particular P-51D in April 1945 to claim most of his ground kills, which eventually totalled 25 and one shared. Thury also had two and one shared aerial victories. *Pauline* (painted in black) had a replacement rudder with a light grey finish.

ABOVE: The 505th FS did not have a rudder colour for added unit identification. *"Mariam"* (painted in black) was P-51D 44-14052 6N-P, which featured three victory symbols above the pin-up girl artwork.

ABOVE: Another successful ground-strafing pilot in the 505th FS was Archie Tower. His last *"Lucky Boy"* (painted in black) was 44-73074 6N-D, and it displayed a red block with swastika markings to record Tower's 18 ground and one and one shared aerial credits. This photograph was taken at a base 'open house' on 1 August 1945.

ABOVE RIGHT: Joe Thury's 44-14656 6N-C photographed in late February 1945 with 12 victories recorded. Applied on several 339th FG Mustangs, these Nazi flags were printed, glued on and varnished over.

RIGHT: *Princess Pat* (44-11325 D7-K) was one of the few Dallas-built P-51Ds to serve with the 339th FG. Note the red rudder adopted by the 503rd FS. Assigned to Phillip Petitt, the aircraft, flown by another pilot, was shot down by an errant B-17 gunner on 7 April 1945!

P-51D-20-NA 44-64148 of the 504th FS/339th FG, Fowlmere, March 1945
Group CO William C Clark took this aircraft as a replacement in late March 1945 following the loss of his previously assigned P-51K 44-11745 *Happy III* on 22 February 1945. The latter aircraft had fallen to flak near Coburg, in Germany, whilst being flown by Capt Ray F Herrmann, who was killed in the incident. As with Clark's other personal Mustangs, 44-64148 was also named *Happy*. *Dotty* on the canopy frame was his wife's name.

Apart from personal adornment, 339th FG Mustangs also had no markings changes other than the introduction of rudder colours during October-November 1944. Similarly, the 352nd FG's markings remained little altered apart from the use of a dark shade of blue for the group marking. This came into use during the late summer or autumn of 1944 when few camouflaged aircraft were still in service. The shade used was probably British Deep Sky Blue, which was similar to Insignia Blue.

Although the 353rd FG had added another row of checkers to the standard two-row P-51 group nose markings upon receiving the type, this was considered insufficient, as the neighbouring 55th FG's green and yellow checkerboard also appeared to be black and yellow in

P-51D-15-NA 44-14882 of the 328th FS/352nd FG, Asche, January 1945
Originally assigned to Lothar Fieg in October 1944 (as a replacement for P-51D 44-13801) and named *Katydid*, this Mustang displays the darker shade of blue introduced by the Group for its nose marking during the summer of that year. 44-14882 was reassigned to another pilot when 66-mission veteran Fieg returned to the US tour-expired in early March 1945. It did not survive for long following Fieg's departure, however, the fighter being lost near Oldenburg, in Germany, through engine failure on 30 March, at which time it was carrying the rather strange moniker *3rd Baser the Second*. The pilot, Lt Frances J McCarthy, was killed in the crash.

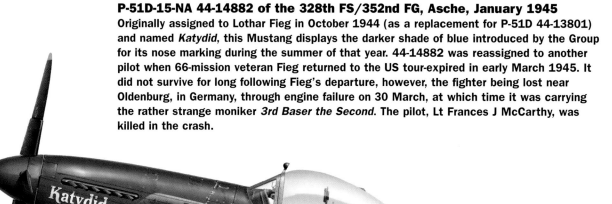

LEFT: The tail number was usually reinstated in black on the red rudder of 328th FS Mustangs when this marking was introduced in November 1944. Due to the shade contrast, it does not show clearly in many photographs, as here on 44-14968 PE-T. Assigned to George Edelen, the name *Momita* was carried on the left side of this P-51D's nose.

BELOW: P-51D 44-63179 PE-R was decorated with red and white 'barber stripes' on the trim tabs, and had a barber pole painted on the right side of the nose – its crew chief had been a barber in civilian life! The Mustang's usual pilot was John Reiners, who had the slogan *Chub A Luk* applied to the left side of the nose.

ABOVE: Pilot Frank Kebelman had a favourite red scarf with white polka dots, and he had the rudder of his P-51D 44-13759 *LONESOME POLECAT* similarly decorated. This aircraft was lost whilst flown by another pilot on 31 December 1944. Note that the blue nose marking has been extended round the canopy frame.

RIGHT: Joseph Mason, CO of the 352nd FG, had his personal Mustangs named *THIS IS IT!* in response to his wife's enquiry about the fighter he flew. This aircraft (P-51D 44-14911 PZ-M) was Mason's last *THIS IS IT!*

THIS PAGE: By 1945, the black and yellow checkerboard on 353rd FG aircraft was uniform in all squadrons, with two rows omitted below the exhaust stacks when a name or slogan was to be painted. Typical examples are these three Mustangs seen landing at Raydon: P-51D 44-15519 LH-H *'Fran' 2nd*, with the yellow rudder of the 350th FS; P-51D 44-14781 YJ-U *"Don Helen"* of the 351st FS, with a plain rudder; and P-51K 44-11624 SX-<u>M</u> *Donna-mite*, with the black rudder of the 352nd FS.

P-51D-5-NA 44-13354 of the 358th FS/355th FG, Steeple Morden, December 1944

The personal P-51D of the 358th FS's commanding officer, Lt Col Emil L Sluga, for eight months, this aircraft was lost on 21 March 1945. Hit by ground fire whilst strafing an airfield near Horsten, in Germany, Sluga was forced to bale out and become a PoW. The aircraft was given the Group's white nose marking when first received in July 1944, the yellow squadron colours being added in November of that year. The fighter's name was derived from the assigned pilot's surname, and it was also Sluga's nickname.

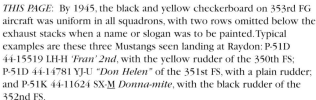

flight. In December 1944 the checkerboard was extended from three to eight squares per longitudinal row, thus plainly distinguishing 353rd from 55th FG Mustangs. Apart from the 350th FS's practice of outlining code letters with yellow, which became common to all squadron aircraft during the final weeks of the war, and the 352nd FS following suit, there were no further notable changes in this group.

When squadron colours were introduced on the tails of 355th FG Mustangs, the Group also painted over the 12-inch wide white nose band in the squadron colour. This left only the spinner in the white group recognition colour. However, the aircraft assigned to the Group CO, Lt Col Ev Stewart, retained an all-white cowling marking, swept down and back to the wing root, and bordered by a six-inch wide red band. The Mustang flown by Stewart's replacement, Lt Col Clay Kinnard, also had an extended white cowling marking (see the colour profile on page 44).

LEFT: The 354th FS P-51D assigned to Norman Fortier during his second tour, displaying a white spinner and red nose band and rudder. The last three figures of the tail number have been repainted in white on the red rudder. The end symbol on the canopy frame is a quarter swastika representing a shared victory.

BELOW: The blue used on 357th FS aircraft was a lighter shade than the blue of the national insignia, as is evident in this photograph of Robert Garlich's 44-14966 *Luscious Lu*.

of the 355th FG, his P-51D ... group commander's aircraft ... wn and back to the wing ... n Stewart moved to ... y 354th FS CO Gordon ... However, it retained the ... und of the photograph ... hed his 44-73144 with an ... der.

P-51D-25-NA 44-73144 of the 354th FS/355th FG, Steeple Morden, April 1945
Eight-kill ace Claiborne H Kinnard's immaculate Mustang was marked with a distinctive white paint scheme on the nose to distinguish it as the mount of the 355th FG's commanding officer. This was Kinnard's fifth personal P-51 whilst flying with the Steeple Morden-based group, all of which featured the WR-A code and were named *Man O'War*.

BELOW: The 356th FG CO's personal P-51D, with its spinner painted with red, yellow and blue four-inch wide spirals to represent all three squadrons. The canopy frame carries the pilot's name in yellow on a red background.

BELOW RIGHT: Hess Bomberger's P-51D 44-15080 QI-B has a blue rudder and blue spinner on which the two-inch red stripes have yet to be completed. This 361st FS aircraft was later named *Carolyn's Vergeltungswaffe*.

C Flight within the 355th FG's 354th FS had always made a point of marking its assigned aircraft with the letter C near the top of the rudder. On aircraft wearing camouflage finish, the C was painted in white, whilst natural metal machines saw the letter applied in black. With the introduction of red rudders, the C was marked flight-wide in white. The other flights within the Squadron also intermittently made use of coloured trim tabs for identification, and after coloured rudders were introduced, there was some use of the letter A by that flight on its aircraft.

Like the 355th, the 356th FG also carried its squadron colours on the noses of its Mustangs during the final months of the war, but in this case on the spinners. The alternating red and blue bands on the spinner took some time to apply, and this may have been one of the reasons for going to a single spinner colour – squadron colours on spinners were introduced in February 1945. An exception was the P-51D flown by group CO, Col Philip Tukey, which had its spinner decorated with a red, yellow and blue spiral. Following the introduction of squadron colours, these were also applied to the lower canopy frame on some aircraft, but by March 1945 this had become common to all P-51s in the 356th.

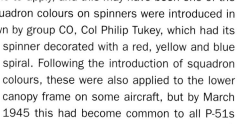

ABOVE: *Texas Terror IV* had similar camouflage to leading 355th FG ace Henry Brown's P-51D (see page 77). Flown by Lee Mendenhall, the Mustang's red trim tab identified its assignment to A Flight of the 354th FS.

LEFT: The 357th FG's 362nd FS had no changes to its recognition markings throughout hostilities. In this photograph, taken in January 1945, the field-camouflaged P-51D (44-14152) was the long-serving mount of William Gruber. P-51D G4-S 44-15607 carries the name *Ticket To Loraine* beneath the exhaust manifold in red. P-51K G4-G 44-11683 is *Man-O-War* and G4-K 44-63195 is *Marymae*. The last identifiable aircraft in the flight is G4-X 44-63199 *TOOLIN' FOOLS' REVENGE*.

RIGHT: In the 357th FG, the bar for barred letters was usually painted above the letter, as on this late P-51D.

ABOVE AND RIGHT: P-51D 44-63195 G4-K was Richard Potter's assigned aircraft. Its name, *Marymae*, is barely visible, having been applied in red below the exhaust manifold. A later photograph shows the beginnings of a piece of girlie art aft of the name.

LEFT: The 363rd FS adopted a red rudder for additional identification. A play of light gives two quite different shades in this photograph but the red was the same red (probably British Roundel Red) as used in the Group nose marking. B6-O is P-51D 44-72187, assigned to Ed Carr, and B6-D is 44-15529, named *Pony's Express* by pilot Frank Kyle for his wife.

ABOVE AND LEFT: John Duncan's G4-Z 44-14612 carried the name *HotShot* on the left side of its nose.

ABOVE: The 357th FG received only a handful of P-51K models, one of which was G4-G 44-11683 *Man-O-War*, named by Ken Hagen.

ABOVE: G4-X 44-63199 and camouflaged G4-D 44-14849 *GASH HOUND* take off from Leiston. The latter machine was assigned to Peter Pelon.

ABOVE: The 364th FS painted its rudders yellow from November 1944, the tail number being reinstated in black. P-51D 44-13621 C5-X *PHILLY-DILLIES* was the personal steed of Stephen Wasylyk.

ABOVE: The significance of an aircraft nickname was often only known to the pilot and his groundcrew. *4 BOLTS* was the strange moniker carried by 44-13783 C5-M. *Rovin' Rhoda* was painted on the left side of the nose.

LEFT: P-51D 44-64099 *ARKANSAS TRAVELLER* was Tom Adam's aircraft. Although it carries five victory symbols, Adams was officially credited with four and a shared in the air. The code C5-L is painted under the left wing, dating this as a post-VE-Day photo.

ABOVE AND RIGHT: Named *Junior Miss II*, B6-L 44-63680 was flown by Glenn Zarnke. B6-R 44-14519 served several pilots and survived hostilities. Both these aircraft show that the squadron continued to use the same stencils for code application as it had done in its early days of operations in the ETO.

The 357th FG was another group that had no markings changes to its P-51s other than the application of squadron colours to rudders.

An extended nose group marking was a feature of 359th FG Mustangs from November 1944. The shade of green used in the application of this marking was also changed, for initially it had been a light grass green. However, with the introduction of natural metal finishes, a darker shade was used. This was probably either the British Dark Green camouflage shade or US Medium Green. The extension of this group marking took it back in a sweep to the end of the exhaust stack and then down and back to terminate under the leading edge of the wing. Prior to the introduction of rudder colours, the group's 368th FS had introduced a practice of painting rudder trim tabs green as an additional squadron recognition feature. Following the adoption of the yellow rudder by this squadron, some of its aircraft had a yellow spiral painted around the green spinner, whilst others had the lower canopy frame painted yellow. The odd 369th and 370th FS Mustang also had the lower canopy frame painted in the squadron colour.

Yellow paintwork on the noses of 361st FG Mustangs was extended rearwards in late July/early August 1944, being taken back over the anti-glare Olive Drab to the end of the engine bay, and then down to a panel line running to the exhaust stack. At the exhaust stack the yellow was taken down and forward under the nose at a point roughly in line with the halfway mark of the exhaust stack. However, the 375th FS went even further by taking the rear part of the yellow marking down to the lower edge of the second long inspection panel. In the final weeks of the war it became common practice for wing tips to be painted in the squadron colour, although examples of this were to be seen during 1944.

Apart from decoration of fin fillets and trim tabs in the 385th FS to distinguish flight leadership, the 364th FG's markings remained little changed. The 479th FG also had no significant development to authorised markings.

Shortly after VE-Day in May 1945, the Eighth Air Force ordered that all its aircraft were to carry identification markings on the underside of the left wing. The reason was the uncautioned exuberance of young pilots in ultra-low flying, bringing an upsurge in accidents and also causing fright and annoyance to many members of the British public, and their livestock. On Mustangs, the 'buzz' markings consisted of the squadron code, a hyphen and the individual letter of the aircraft. Painted in black on metal finish and yellow on camouflage greys, the characters were 36 inches high. On those aircraft belonging to units that had not been issued with SD 110 codes, the markings were usually an abbreviated form of the unit designation, followed by a number or letter.

P-51D-15-NA 44-15007 of the 369th FS/359th FG, East Wretham, December 1944
Delivered to the 359th FG at East Wretham as an attrition replacement in November 1944, this aircraft featured the swept back and down medium green nose marking and the red rudder that identified the 369th FS from the middle of that month until war's end. Its regular pilot was Thomas J Klem.

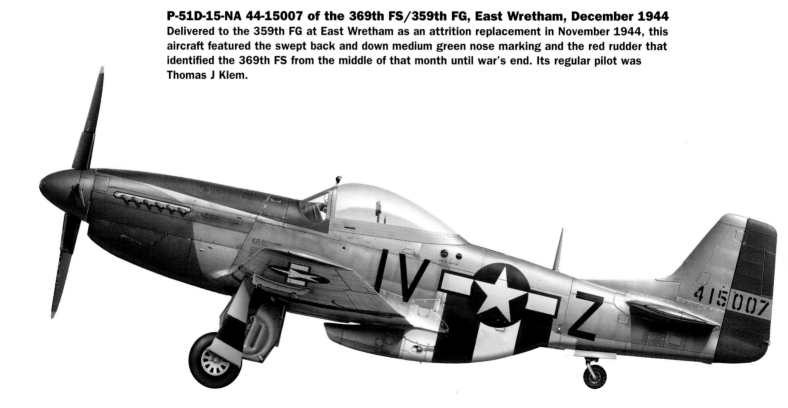

RIGHT: In the 369th FS, tail numbers were reinstated or painted around on red rudders. P-51D 44-14543 IV-P was *PRECIOUS PAT* (in red with white outline), whilst the other unnamed aircraft are 44-15007 IV-Z and 44-15394 IV-D, the last being lost on 21 March 1945.

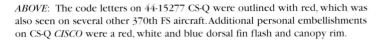

ABOVE: The code letters on 44-15277 CS-Q were outlined with red, which was also seen on several other 370th FS aircraft. Additional personal embellishments on CS-Q *CISCO* were a red, white and blue dorsal fin flash and canopy rim.

ABOVE: This line-up shot of 370th FS Mustangs at East Wretham shows that the black type identity bands were retained on horizontal tail surfaces and wings – in fact those on 44-14979 CS-H were outlined in red. This aircraft was named *Little Dixie* (in yellow) and the next in line, 44-72208 CS-C, carries the name *DELECTABLE* on the nose (in white).

RIGHT: The green nose of 359th FG Mustangs was extended rearwards in November 1944 with a sweep down to the rear of the exhaust manifold and then to the wing root. The blue used for the rudder colour of 370th FS aircraft was Insignia Blue or an equivalent. It was usual not to overpaint the tail number as seen on 44-13893 CS-E, which was named *Caroline*.

BELOW: Two 376th FS Mustangs with yellow rudders and, in the case of the P-51D, a yellow canopy frame. The P-51C marked WW ('War-Weary' and thus unfit for further combat) is a training aircraft. The tail number on the fin has been repainted at some point to include the full serial, 43-25044.

RIGHT: A flight of 376th FS Mustangs shows variations in markings. Leading is William Sykes' *Wilma Lee* (44-14520 E9-S) with a coloured trim tab. Next is 44-14600 E9-V *Curiosity Betty II* with standard paintwork, then James Smith's *Daisy Mae III* (44-14514 E9-Y), whose yellow nose marking has not been taken over the olive drab anti-glare panel, and lastly P-51B 42-106538 E9-A with a black WW on the fin, indicating that it was a training aircraft. This last aircraft was once assigned to ace Dale Spencer.

ABOVE: When the red rudder was introduced on 374th FS aircraft, a band was left unpainted where the tail number was situated. B7-O 44-14957 *DARLIN' DORA* also has red wing tips and canopy frame, it becoming usual for these embellishments to be applied to all squadron aircraft. Finally, the letter O appears to be intersected by a diagonally placed black bar.

RIGHT: The yellow nose on Homer Powell's *'Gay' Crusader* (44-15752 E9-P) extended further down the engine compartment panel than was usual for this marking.

The 361st FG's extended yellow nose marking was introduced in late July 1944, squadron colours on rudders in November and on wing tips and canopy frames during January-February 1945. The remaining black type identity bands were removed from most aircraft by the following spring. P-51D 44-15036 has an ace of spades motif on a lower nose panel. Jerome Moore was usually associated with this Mustang during wartime, but another pilot was in the cockpit when it was destroyed in a post-war accident. The fighter is seen in formation with the group's Vultee Vengeance hack.

P-51D-15-NA 44-15036 of the 374th FS/361st FG, Chievres, March 1945
A replacement aircraft received by the 374th FS in November 1944, this Mustang was involved in a fatal accident on 4 January 1945, the pilot, Lt John R Wilson, being killed.

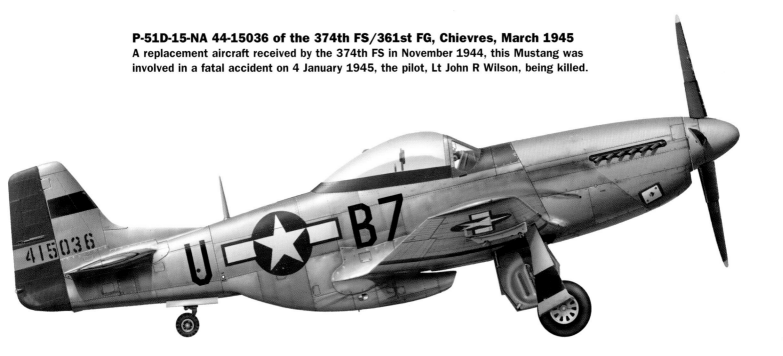

RIGHT: A flight of 434th FS Mustangs with their tail numbers reinstated. Most 479th FG P-51s had their tail numbers removed in the final months of the war, although it appears that an order to reinstate them was forthcoming before the end of hostilities. The second aircraft is 44-14523 L2-K, which is also featured in the photograph below. The titling *The ONLEY Genevieve IV* is carried on the canopy frame of 44-14395 L2-M, this type of personal marking being a common practice in this squadron, for it allowed the canopy and its name to be removed to a replacement aircraft. This particular P-51D was assigned to Robert Kline.

LEFT: P-51D 44-14523 L2-K *The YAKIMA Chief*, assigned to Harold Stotts, has still to have its tail number reinstated.

RIGHT: P-51D 44-14355 enjoyed only a short life with the 479th FG, suffering engine failure on 27 September 1944. Assigned to Claire Duffie, and coded L2-A-, it was unusual in having a red flight leader's band around the rear fuselage.

ABOVE, RIGHT AND BELOW: This series of photographs, featuring other 434th FS aircraft, was taken by Robert Kline. P-51D 44-14423 L2-O *BOOMERANG JR* was Arthur Jefferies' mount. P-51D 44-72336 L2-R *Setonia No 3* was assigned to Donald Pierce and P-51D 44-14846 L2-S *Pauline* was flown by Donald Stott – this was the only one of the trio to retain its tail number.

ABOVE AND ABOVE RIGHT: As previously mentioned, the canopy frame was a favoured place for names on 434th FS Mustangs, as this could be transferred to a replacement aircraft, thus avoiding the need to repaint the name. The *IMPATIENT VIRGIN* graced L2-Z 44-63176, which was at one time assigned to William Daudistel. *THE Flying DUTCHMAN* was allegedly on the right side of 44-63176's canopy, but this seems doubtful in view of the contrast in the hand painted codes.

LEFT: A trio of yellow-ruddered 435th FS P-51Ds. J2-G 44-15263 has lost its tail number completely, and J2-N and J2-J have only the last three digits left. These two are 44-14827 and 44-15236 *Roarin' Rose* respectively.

BELOW: The fuselage codes used on 436th FS Mustangs were initially made with the same 18-inch stencils as used on the unit's P-38s. The black and white checkerboard rudder was short-lived, quickly being replaced by a solid black, which was less time consuming to apply.

Operational Training Units

In January 1944 the 555th Fighter Training Squadron (FTS) came into being at Goxhill, in Lincolnshire, as the operational training unit for pilots arriving in the ETO. Mustangs being in short supply, the unit was the recipient of cast-offs from operational units. Issued the SD 110 code combination C7, the unit painted this marking in the standard size and location on the fuselages of its aircraft, white on camouflage finish and black on natural metal. Type identity bands were carried, and where these had been removed by operational units they were often repainted. Allied Expeditionary Air Force (AEAF) stripes were not carried, and were removed from aircraft received with these markings in place. 555th FTS Mustangs were to be seen with a variety of nose markings, including checkerboards, possibly retained from their previous operational units.

In the autumn of 1944 it was decided to form an Operational Training Unit (OTU) in each operational fighter group. The reasoning behind this move was that each combat group had its own individual procedures, and replacement pilots would be better served learning these from the outset of their commitment to flying in the ETO. As a result, in October 1944 each fighter squadron was issued with three war-weary aircraft of the type flown, although the number on hand appears to have fluctuated between three and five.

Most groups gave their OTU aircraft special markings. For example, 4th FG OTU aircraft had their rudders painted red, white and blue in three roughly equal horizontal sections, red at the top and blue at the bottom. Additionally, the individual identities of these aircraft were marked by numerals instead of letters. The numbers used were 2, 3 and 4 in each squadron, marked 24 inches high in black or white, depending on the aircraft finish, and placed, as with letters, on the rear fuselage. Two of the training P-51Bs had a passenger seat installed behind the pilot. Later still, the aircraft coded VF-4 was painted deep sky blue overall and P-51B WD-2 finished in red.

BELOW RIGHT: When photographed in March 1945 following its 'in-the-field' conversion into the 4th FG's first two-seat Mustang, this aircraft (P-51B 43-12193) had already completed a long tour in the front line with the 335th FS. Boasting a unique code to denote its dual capacity, the former fighter was used by the group's 'Clobber College' Operational Training Unit.

BELOW: The chief architect in the modification of P-51B 43-12193 into a 'two-holer' was the 335th FS's senior technical inspector, T/Sgt 'Woody' Jensen, who is seen here sat in the aircraft's front cockpit. Crouching on the wing is the 4th FG's engineering officer, Capt Grunow – the third individual in this photo remains unidentified. Note how the glazing for the Mustang is provided by two standard P-51B canopies.

BELOW: Although initially flown in natural metal, 43-12193 was eventually repainted in 4th FG red overall, with the aircraft's codes and WW marking applied in the same shade of blue as the national insignia and the rudder markings. Late war 336th FS pilot Lt William Hastings is seen here posing with the veteran fighter.

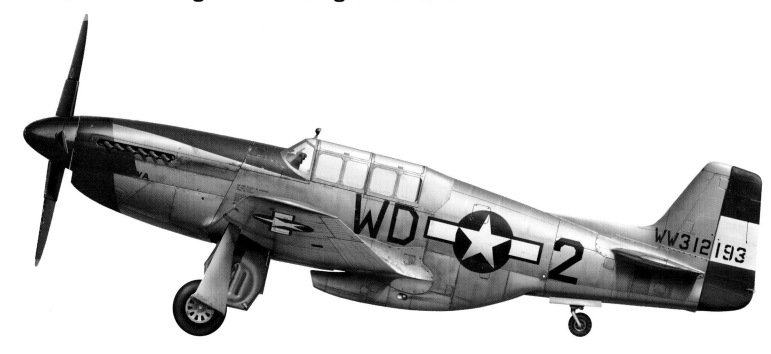

P-51B-1-NA 43-12193 of the 335th FS/4th FG OTU, Debden, April 1945
Converted at Debden to take a passenger, this was one of the oldest Merlin Mustangs still flying in Europe by war's end. It had entered service with the 354th FG in late 1943, and later served with the 555th FTS at Goxhill, before being passed on to the 4th FG's 335th FS. The veteran fighter was eventually relegated to the group's operational training unit.

The OTU aircraft employed by the 20th FG were less distinguished. Whereas the Group's combat aircraft had the front portion of their spinners painted white, the training aircraft were identified by an all-black spinner. Individual identities mostly took the form of barred letters, and the WW (War-Weary, which indicated that the aircraft was time-expired, and therefore unfit for further combat) marking was painted in white on the geometric device on the tail. Otherwise, markings were as worn by the Group's combat Mustangs.

In the 55th FG, groundcrews had a much more demanding scheme to apply to the group's OTU aircraft – the Mustangs' rudders were covered with six-inch squares of green and yellow checkerboard. Again, numerals were used for individual identities, 1 to 4 for the 38th FS, 5 to 8 for the 338th and 9 to 12 for the 343rd, although following losses, the numbers used appear to have been assigned without regard to squadron order. As well as being painted in the usual individual aircraft identity position aft of the national insignia, the number was also applied forward of the cockpit to the rear of the engine bay on the fuselage side.

By contrast, 78th FG OTU aircraft featured no special markings other than the WW on the tail fin. Individual letters were both barred and unbarred, and assigned where needed. Like the 4th FG, the 78th had a two-seat P-51B conversion, which was painted red overall in the final months of the war in the ETO. All three of the squadrons within the 339th FG painted the rudders of their OTU aircraft yellow. Random letters were used and the WW marking carried on fins or rudders. The 352nd FG OTU aircraft were identified by numerals 2, 3 and 4 painted on their fin in the 486th FS, whereas the other two squadrons used barred letters and the WW marking.

The 353rd FG's trio of squadrons each had OTU aircraft marked with numerals starting with 2. It appears that replacements were given a higher number, however, as the 350th FS is known to have had P-51s marked LH-7, LH-8 and LH-9 in service after VE-Day. The 355th FG's OTU Mustangs were at one time identified by having their individual letter framed by a rectangular box outline. Later, OTU aircraft had their rudders painted black. No special markings have come to light for the 356th FG's trainers other than the WW suffix or prefix to the tail number. The 357th FG's OTU Mustangs employed numeral identification, with the run of numbers being

ABOVE: OTU aircraft in the 20th FG boasted all black spinners in contrast to the group's front line P-51s, which had the tips of their spinners left in natural metal. Note the addition of the WW 'war weary' marking within the Group's distinctive geometric device on the tail of this tired P-51B.

ABOVE AND RIGHT: Mustang trainers in the 364th FG were identified by numbers on the geometric shapes. The 55th FG also used numerals, repeating them on the forward fuselage. A yellow and green checkerboard rudder was the main identifying marking for its trainers. P-51B 43-12438 was written off in this crash-landing on 12 September 1944.

ABOVE: All fighter groups had a two-seat conversion for training in the final months of the war. P-51B 42-106826 was a 78th FG conversion that was at first painted overall red, although it was reputedly overall blue by the time this photograph was taken.

P-51B-5-NA 43-6928 of the 343rd FS/55th FG Group OTU, Wormingford, April 1945
Following operational service with the 355th FG (where it was assigned to 11.5-kill ace William Hovde of the 358th FS), this P-51B was passed on to the 496th FTG before being issued to the 55th FG for operational training purposes. It was damaged in a taxiing accident in April 1945 but was apparently repaired, as it was not declared salvage until after the summer of that year. Originally flown in camouflage finish, all paint was removed at some point in the aircraft's long career in the ETO. Note that the fighter's serial number was reapplied incorrectly on the tail as 36529 instead of 36928!

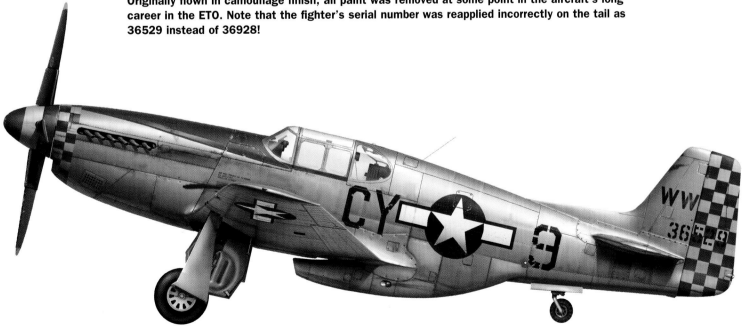

allotted on a group rather than squadron basis, and with no duplications. The 359th FG was another outfit that had no special markings other than the WW letters on the tail. However, its OTU aircraft were mostly, if not all, identified by barred letters. The 361st FG also had no special distinguishing markings for its trainers other than WW.

Numerals were used by the 364th FG apparently on a group basis, as high numbers were to be seen serving in each squadron, some reaching to the twenties. As with its letters, the unit's numbers were painted in white on the 364th's distinctive geometric tail devices. While it is known that the 434th FS of the 479th FG used numerals (2, 3 and 4 being noted), the 435th and 436th FSs appear to have preferred the use of barred letters on their trainers. A two-seat conversion used by the group – 43-6865 J2-Q – was painted yellow overall in the spring of 1945.

ABOVE: Operational training aircraft in the 357th FG were usually distinguished by numerals for plane-in-squadron identification.

Scouting Force Mustangs

In August 1944 Lt Gen James H Doolittle, Commander Eighth Air Force, authorised the formation of weather scouting units in each of the three bomb divisions. Equipped with Mustangs, these units were specifically tasked with flying ahead of a bomber task force and reporting up-to-the-minute local weather conditions back to the 'heavies' by radio. The aircraft used for these flights were provided by the resident fighter group on whose station the weather scouting unit was based, namely the 364th FG at Honington for the 1st Division, the 355th FG at Steeple Morden for the 2nd and the 55th FG at Wormingford for the 3rd. Pilot strength for each unit was eight, and eventually the fighter groups involved received an additional six Mustangs to add to their normal complement. The weather aircraft within each fighter group were distinguished by special markings additional to the group's normal markings.

Mustangs of the 1st Scouting Force were attached to the 385th FS at Honington, and each carried the 5E code of that unit on the rear fuselage. The individual plane-in-unit letter was carried on the fin in black, the squadron's triangle marking not being applicable to these aircraft. In September 1944, a few weeks after the unit had been established at Honington, additional markings were authorised. The spinner was painted red and a 12-inch wide white nose band applied directly aft of it. A three-inch wide red band was painted around the top and bottom edges of both vertical and horizontal tail surfaces. However, some P-51s with the red spinner and tail outline still retained the blue and white nose band.

P-51D-10-NA 44-14375 of the 1st Scouting Force, Honington, December 1944
Although the 1st Scouting Force was allocated a distinctive marking consisting of a red spinner and white nose band, some of the aircraft obtained from the 364th FG continued to carry that unit's blue and white nose band. Declared salvage after an emergency landing at a Continental airfield in December 1944, this Mustang was strafed by *Luftwaffe* fighters on New Year's Day 1945 whilst awaiting final disposal.

LEFT: A red spinner, white nose band and red border to the empennage marked 1st Scouting Force Mustangs. This unit had become the 857th Bomb Squadron by the time this photograph of 9H-Y, crash-landed at Bassingbourn, was taken.

BELOW LEFT AND RIGHT: Experimental 2nd Scouting Force Mustangs had the bar painted below the squadron code, as on 44-13709 YF-H. Later 2nd Scouting Force Mustangs had the bar above the code, as with YF-M 414524 *Lil LARRY II*. The nose bands remained white in contrast to the bright colours used by other Steeple Morden squadrons.

In March 1945 the 1st Scouting Force became regularised as the 857th BS, a designation that had become vacant when the former *Carpetbagger* B-24 unit had been disbanded. The colour markings remained unchanged, although the unit's 5E code was replaced by the 857th's 9H code, painted in black and positioned in the same location as the former 5E.

When the 2nd Scouting Force was established at Steeple Morden in August 1944, its assigned P-51Ds, distributed among the three fighter squadrons for maintenance, were given code letters appropriate to the squadron maintaining them. Their only distinction from the fighter Mustangs of the same squadron was a bar painted under the squadron code letters,

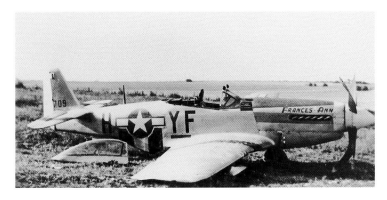

P-51D-5-NT 44-11341 of the 2nd Scouting Force, Steeple Morden, December 1944
2nd Scouting Force aircraft were distinguished from other Steeple Morden-based Mustangs by the black bar painted above or below the squadron two-letter code of the unit to which they were assigned for maintenance. Originally, the bar was painted below the code, but most aircraft subsequently had it applied above the code where it was more easily seen. When the 355th FG adopted coloured rudders and nose bands as additional means of squadron identification, the Scouting Force aircraft became visually more distinguishable in that they retained the all-white nose markings and had no coloured rudders. Assigned to George Ceglarski, *SWEET STUFF* was damaged in a belly-landing on 26 November 1944, and although repaired, it was well and truly wrecked in another accident at Steeple Morden on 8 January 1945.

indicating the second unit in much the same way as a bar under an individual aircraft letter indicated the second airframe with that letter in a squadron. The bar was black, four inches wide and approximately 30 inches long.

When the 355th FG commenced painting the rudders of its Mustangs with squadron colours (nose bands were also applied) in October 1944, the scouting force aircraft retained their white

ABOVE: 3rd Scouting Force Mustangs had normal 55th FG decor apart from the vertical tail. The fin had a red leading edge and the rudder a red and white checkerboard.

spinners and nose bands and colourless rudders. Around the same time the black bar was painted above the squadron code on replacement aircraft, where it was more visible than when applied below.

At first, the P-51Ds provided for 3rd Scouting Force use had no special identifying markings. Like the 2nd Scouting Force machines, these aircraft were distributed among the three fighter squadrons within the 55th FG. In December 1944 identifying markings were applied to the tails of the Mustangs, these taking the form of a red checkerboard made up of six-inch squares painted directly onto the existing finish or a white ground. Additionally, a four-inch wide stripe was painted down the leading edge of the fin so that two inches were visible on each side of the vertical surface when viewed in profile. In mid-February 1945 the 3rd Scouting Force was given squadron status as the 862nd BS. However, there was no change in markings to acknowledge this development.

Special Mustang Assignments

The vulnerability of unarmed, camera-carrying F-5 Lightning reconnaissance aircraft to interception by enemy fighters, particularly jets, led to the 7th Photographic Reconnaissance Group (PRG) being given a number of P-51D/Ks for escort duties. First received in January 1945, these Mustangs were adorned with the group colours – a dark blue spinner and a 63-inch by 12-inch red band painted under the engine exhaust stacks. Each of the photographic squadrons had four aircraft, and they applied a particular colour to rudders; red for the 13th

P-51D-25-NA 44-72419 of the 14th Photographic Reconnaissance Squadron/ 7th Photographic Reconnaissance Group, Chalgrove, April 1945
This was one of a handful of Mustangs allocated to the 7th PRG in March 1945 for use as fighter escorts for the group's camera-equipped F-5 Lightnings. Given similar colour markings to those then in use on the F-5s, no individual aircraft identities were displayed other than the tail numbers.

PRS aircraft, dark green for those of the 14th, white for the 22nd and blue for the 27th. No fuselage code letters were carried.

The three fighter wings also maintained small flights of aircraft for use by headquarters officers, and these included Mustangs within their ranks. The 65th Fighter Wing (FW), which stationed its flight at Debden, had a nose marking of three white and two red encircling bands. The P-51B operated by this unit – 43-6542 – had all of its camouflage removed and the letters J-A applied on the fuselage. It is not known if this was an SD 110 code split either side of the national insignia or the initial letters of the Wing's commanding general, Jesse Auton. All 65th FW fighter types carried this marking. The Mustang's spinner was painted white, with a red spiral thereon. The width of the red and white nose bands was approximately eight inches.

The 66th FW marking on its aircraft, stationed at Duxford or nearby Fowlmere, was based on its groups' widespread use of the checkerboard. A most elaborate design, the engine cowling was covered with varying rows of red, white, green, yellow and black six-inch squares. This decor was worn by P-51D 44-13590, named *Piccadilly Prince III*, and later by P-51K 44-11660 *Rachel-H 2nd*. No fuselage codes were carried.

ABOVE: The fighter wing headquarters had a few aircraft assigned for officer use, including P-51K 44-11660, which was used by the 66th Fighter Wing. The fighter was adorned with a checkerboard composed of red, yellow, white, green and black squares. The rudder was black, as was the name *Rachel-H 2nd*.

Single Mustangs were also operated by other Eighth Air Force organisations. The 495th Fighter Training Group had a P-51B in silver finish, with a green spinner and nose band, for use by Maj Gen Bill Kepner, Commander of VIII Fighter Command. The Air Technical Section of VIII Fighter Command at Bovingdon had several Mustangs for experimental purposes, including assigned P-51B 43-12425 VQ-C, which was in hand for several months. Its codes conformed to the norm for Mustang sizes and colours. P-51D 44-13730 was also among the several different types operated by 'A' Flight of the Eighth Air Force Headquarters Squadron. A bare metal machine, it boasted a black E aft of the fuselage national insignia. This Mustang was at times flown by Gen Doolittle.

Following the end of hostilities, several other headquarters gained the use of the odd Mustang, and by far the most colourful of these was War-Weary P-51D 44-13885, flown by the 4th Combat Bomb Wing at Bury St Edmunds. Modified to take a passenger, it had an all-yellow empennage in line with the wing's B-17s, and a red spinner backed by broad cowling bands of red, white and blue.

Auxiliary Fuel Tanks

During the spring of 1944 the Allied fighter force achieved air supremacy in the sky over North-West Europe. VIII Fighter Command Mustangs were the primary force responsible for this achievement through this fighter having a radius of action of nearly 400 miles on its internal fuel tanks. With the addition of disposable auxiliary fuel tanks, commonly called drop tanks, the P-51s could escort the bombers to any target in Europe. Drop tanks soon became a familiar appendage under Mustang wings.

The first type used was a tank originally designed for fitment to the P-39 Airacobra. Known as a 75-gallon tank, it was teardrop shaped and painted overall Neutral Gray, with the filler cap in red and instructional details in black. This became the main tank used by P-51s until the spring of 1944, when British-made sheet metal fabrications in a cigar shape, known as 108-gallon tanks, came into use. These were painted light grey or medium grey overall, depending on supplies, to accord with aircraft undersurface colours. On some later production metal tanks the support bands at the attachment points were also painted red.

During 1944 sheet metal tanks, rated as 110 gallons, arrived from the USA, and these were used exclusively by P-51s while supplies lasted. Again, these were teardrop shaped and finished in silver, with red filler points.

The most used tank by VIII Fighter Command was the so-called 'paper' tank, a lightweight plastic/paper composition tank rated as 108 gallons and shaped much as the steel tanks of this capacity. These were silver finished, with the bands at attachment points painted red.

LEFT: An early 357th FS P-51B with 52 sortie symbols – an uncommon practice on Mustangs. The upper half of the D-Day stripes on the fuselage have been painted out with dark green and the code letters refreshed. Drop tanks beneath the wing are silver 108-US gallon types. This aircraft was assigned to Harold Hoffman but was lost whilst being flown by another pilot on 2 August 1944.

BELOW: Hugging 108-gallon 'paper' drop tanks, the 20th FG's *"Little Lady"* (in red) 44-13715 KI-K is run-up by its crew chief. For expediency, on some aircraft – this one for example – within the 20th, the white of the group marking was omitted, the bare metal being used instead for contrast.

P-51D-5-NA 44-13692 of the 77th FS/20th FG, Kings Cliffe, December 1944
This aircraft features the distinctive, extended 20th FG group nose marking of black and white bars as applied in October 1944. Delivered to the Squadron in July 1944, this Mustang was assigned to Richard J Dempsey, who named it *Mary D*. When Dempsey finished his tour in December, the aircraft was taken over by Cartheledge L Huey Jr, who had the fighter renamed *Maggie* on the left side of the nose and *Sandy* on the right.

LEFT: Typical examples of personal fuselage art and mission victories can be seen on Lt Ralph Hofer's P-51B 42-106924 QP-L. No fewer than 17 black and white Luftwaffe crosses, a train and two sailing ships are marked onto the Mustang, denoting Hofer's success against the enemy in 1943-44. The words *Salem Representative* were reportedly applied in yellow outlined with black.

Personal Markings

A feature of many Eighth Air Force fighters were the motifs, nicknames and other inscriptions painted on the forward fuselage by pilots or groundcrews. In most cases the aircraft was given a name by the pilot, although occasionally the name was suggested by the crew chief or another mechanic. Sometimes two names were applied, contributed by both pilot and groundcrew. Popular were the first names of wives or sweethearts so that a photograph of this inscription could be taken and sent to the lady concerned. There were cases of a pilot having one female name on the left side of the fuselage and another female name on the right side! Sometimes the pilot permitted the crew chief or his assistant to apply the name of their wife or girlfriend.

Normally, there were more pilots than aircraft in a squadron, which led to aircraft assignments being shared, and to different names appearing on each side of the fuselage. When a pilot finished his tour and the fighter was assigned to a replacement pilot, the names and personal decorations were usually changed.

Although the assigned pilot had first say in the matter of personal decor, groundcrews were usually responsible for the minor embellishments. A tally of the sorties flown by the aircraft was kept by some crews on their charges, each mission being represented by either a broom (for fighter sweeps), an umbrella (for escort top cover) or a vertical bomb silhouette (for fighter-bomber work or general missions), each of these symbols usually being applied in black. However, this form of record became very rare on Mustangs from the spring of 1944 onwards.

A pilot's victories were recorded as swastikas, crosses or Nazi flags, usually below the left side of the cockpit. After Eighth Air Force HQ decreed that ground-strafing victories should rate equal to those obtained in air combat due to the great danger faced in obtaining the former, there was generally no distinction made between ground and air credits as painted on aircraft.

On most assigned fighters it was usual to have the pilot's name and rank, and that of the groundcrew, on a small painted panel forward of the cockpit on the left side. With the P-51D and K models, these details were often painted on the cockpit canopy frame itself.

LEFT: A close up of the highly detailed nose art that adorned 'Cowboy' Megura's P-51B 43-6636. This 4th FG aircraft was lost to German flak on 9 May 1944 during a strafing attack on Reims/ Champagne airfield, its pilot, 1Lt Vernon 'Cub' Burroughs, being made a PoW.

ABOVE: The 350th FS outlined its code letters with yellow, as can be seen on Don Kammer's *"Baltimore Belle"* (black and yellow) 44-72096 LH-F. This practice was not so widespread in the 353rd FG's remaining two squadrons.

LEFT: Capt John Francis 'Smiling Jack' Thornell poses with his crew chief, S/Sgt G A McIndoo, and their P-51B-15 42-106872 of the 328th FS/352nd FG in late June 1944. Thornell scored 17.25 aerial victories between 30 January and 21 June 1944, claiming no fewer than 11 of these kills in this very Mustang. He was also credited with damaging two aircraft and destroying two in strafing attacks. Note the fighter's highly-prized Spitfire rear-view mirror that helped compensate for the B-model's lack of rearward visibility.

The Aces

Some pilots were undoubtedly more able and aggressive in combat than others, but the popular distinction of 'ace' is probably unjustified. As many fighter pilots have acknowledged, being in the right place at the right time is crucial to success, and that surprise is paramount. The speculation that only one out of every ten enemy fighter pilots shot down knew that he was about to be attacked is also valid. Moreover, it seems grossly unfair to label a pilot with five aerial victories an ace, while one with four has no such accolade. Yet ace status based on five aerial victories has been accepted since its origin with French combatants during the First World War, and it remains a yardstick in assessing fighter pilot prowess.

The Eighth Air Force had more fighter aces than any other branch of the United States military during the Second World War, and most achieved this fame flying Mustangs. Shooting down an enemy aircraft was often far from a precise business, and in many instances the evidence available – pilots' reports and gun camera film – was not always conclusive. The scores of individual pilots, and the overall totals of the fighter units, were subject to review at different command levels throughout the operational period and since, resulting in varying figures being published. Those now generally accepted were contained in the 1985 USAF Office of History Study No 85, with some more recent amendments.

The Eighth Air Force is credited with producing 275 aces, and of these 164 shot down five or more enemy aircraft while flying P-51s. The highest number, 42, served with the 357th FG, the first VIII Fighter Command Mustang unit to become operational. Next in line was the 4th FG with 25, the 352nd with 22, the 355th with 17, the 55th and 339th both with ten, the 359th with nine, the 364th with seven, the 361st with six, 353rd with five, 479th with four and the 20th and 356th with three each. The 78th FG, being the last to convert to the Mustang, had no pilots achieve five victories while flying the type. Although not having an interceptor mission, the 2nd Scouting Force produced one Mustang ace.

In the following listings the P-51s quoted are those known to have been assigned to ace pilots, although many other aircraft remain unidentified. The names given are the main names worn by these machines where more than one was carried. Date abbreviations are in the international form of day, month, year as used in wartime.

BELOW: One of the most flamboyant characters to fly with VIII Fighter Command was Ralph 'Kid' Hofer, who joined the Royal Canadian Air Force prior to America's entry into the war. He was amongst the first 4th FG pilots to 'make ace' with the Mustang in the ETO, scoring six of his eventual 15 kills in this P-51B-15 (42-106924), which he named *Salem Representative* in honour of his home town in Missouri. He is seen here with the 334th FS's orphan dog, 'Duke', which adopted Hofer. Note the ace's non-regulation long hair and lucky college football jersey, which he religiously wore on every sortie. This official USAAF photograph was taken at Debden on 14 May 1944.

4th FG

The 4th FG's most successful P-51 pilot was Ralph K Hofer who is credited with 14 aerial victories. He also scored one kill flying a P-47, and had 14 strafing credits for enemy aircraft destroyed on the ground. A former RAF pilot, Hofer was the only high-scoring ace in the Eighth Air Force to be shot down and killed in air combat, the ace meeting his demise over Mostar, in Yugoslavia, on 2 July 1944. His personal P-51Bs were 43-6946 QP-L and 42-106924 QP-L, named *Salem Representative*.

LEFT: Aces High! Nine pilots from the 336th FS were credited with five or more kills during the Second World War, and the four highest scorers are all seen in this posed group shot, taken in March 1944. At the extreme left is Johnny Godfrey, who claimed 16.333 kills, then comes Don Gentile with 21.833 (two of these victories were scored with the RAF). Next to him is Peter Lehmann, son of Herbert Lehmann, Director of the US Office of Foreign Relief and former Governor of New York. Lehmann junior was killed on 31 March when his P-51B spun in during a low-level mock dogfight near Duxford, his aircraft suffering a violent centre of gravity change when the fuel load in its 65-gallon upright tank suddenly shifted due to the pilot's aggressive manoeuvring. Next to Lehmann is James Goodson, who scored 14 kills, and Willard Millikan, who claimed 13.

RIGHT: John Godfrey reputedly had the 'sharpest' eyes in the 4th FG, which goes a long way to explaining his success in action in 1943-44. Aside from his 15 and three shared aerial victories, he was also credited with the destruction of 12.666 aircraft on the ground. And like most VIII Fighter Command aces brought down in action, it was his passion for strafing that would prove his downfall. However, Godfrey was not hit by flak in his P-51D on 24 August 1944. Instead, his fighter was terminally damaged by machine gun fire from his wingman, Lt Melvin Dickey! Godfrey had destroyed four Ju 52/3ms at an airfield at Nordhausen just prior to his untimely demise.

LEFT: Wearing his crumpled '50 mission crush' Class A cap, 1Lt John T Godfrey poses on the wing of his P-51B-5 (43-6765) with his crew chief and his dog in early April 1944. Usually flying as a dual scoring element with squadronmate Don Gentile, Godfrey had his Mustang identically marked with red and white checkers to aid in forming up when airborne. Their partnership was the most productive in the 4th FG, for on 8 March they claimed six Bf 109s, followed by three more on the 23rd of that month and 4.333 kills (three Fw 190s, a Bf 109 and 0.333 of a He 111) six days later.

John T Godfrey shot down 13 and shared in the destruction of two other enemy aircraft while flying Mustangs. He had two victories and a shared flying P-47s and 12 plus a shared while ground-strafing. His assigned Mustangs were 43-6765 VF-P and 42-106730 VF-P *Reggie's Reply* during his first tour. On 24 August 1944, whilst on his second tour, Godfrey was accidentally shot down by his wingman during a strafing attack on Nordhausen airfield. He was quickly captured, and remained a PoW until war's end.

Don S Gentile earned much wartime fame as the 4th FG's most successful ace, claiming 21 and two shared victories. Of these, 13 and a shared were obtained in the P-51B, four and a shared with the P-47 and two with the Spitfire V whilst Gentile was serving with the RAF. He also had six strafing credits. Gentile's P-51B, 43-6913 VF-T *Shangri-La,* carried a block of red and white checkerboard below the engine exhaust stacks, as did John Godfrey's P-51B when these pilots flew as leader and wingman.

George Carpenter scored 12 and two shared kills in Mustangs, plus a lone victory in the P-47. He also had four strafing credits. Carpenter used P-51B 43-6575 WD-I *Virginia* to achieve eight of his victories, and was eventually shot down and captured on 18 April 1944 while flying 42-106675 WD-I.

Howard D Hively had 11 credits while flying a Mustang and one with a Thunderbolt. He flew two tours with the 334th FS and became its CO, his assigned Mustangs being 43-6898 QP-J and 44-15347 QP-J.

Nicholas Megura shot down ten enemy aircraft and shared in the destruction of four others, mainly flying P-51B 43-6636 QP-N *Ill Wind*. His combat career was terminated when he had to seek refuge in Sweden with an ailing Mustang on 22 May 1944.

Fred W Glover also claimed ten victories and a shared, as well as 12 strafing kills. He flew 43-12214 VF-C *Rebel Queen* and later 44-14787 VF-B. Ted E Lines was yet another to down ten enemy aircraft, nine of which were claimed while flying his assigned P-51D 44-13555 WD-D. Another 4th FG pilot with ten in Mustangs was Willard W Millikan, who also had three credits while flying P-47s. His personal P-51Bs were 43-6997 VF-U and, later, 43-24769 VF-U *Missouri Mauler*, in which he was shot down on 30 May 1944 and taken prisoner.

Another pilot from the same squadron who ended up in a prison camp as a result of strafing, this time on 20 June 1944, was James A Goodson, who had nine air credits in Mustangs and five in P-47s, and had also destroyed 15 enemy aircraft on the ground. Goodson's Mustangs were 43-6895, 43-7059, 43-24848, 44-13300 and 44-13303, all coded VF-B. Louis H Norley also had nine aerial victories in Mustangs plus one and a shared while in Thunderbolts. P-51Bs assigned to him during his first tour were 43-12416, 43-6802 and 43-6666, all coded VF-O. P-51Ds in his second tour included 44-14435 WD-O and 44-15028 WD-O.

BELOW: One of Ralph 'Kid' Hofer's contemporaries in the 334th FS was Nicholas 'Cowboy' Megura who, like the 'Kid', had been trained by the Canadians. Another to enjoy early success with the Mustang, Megura was credited with 11.833 kills and six damaged between 4 March and 22 May 1944. His promising combat career was cut short on the latter date when his Mustang (43-7158) was shot up in error by an over-zealous P-38 pilot. With his glycol tank seriously holed, Megura was forced to crash-land in neutral Sweden, where he was interned until 28 June.

CAPTAIN DUANE W BEESON
334th FS/4th FG
March 1944

Probably the best thing to say on tactics is that they do alter, and depend entirely on each situation as it exists at the moment. The only rules that can be laid out for actual combat are pretty general, and it just takes plain common sense to apply them at the right time.

I think that the most important one thing to a fighter pilot is speed! The faster an aircraft is moving when he spots an enemy aircraft, the sooner he will be able to take the bounce and get to the Hun. And it's harder for him to bounce you if you are going fast. Of course, keeping a high speed in formations is very hard because the formation falls apart, and also because of trying to save gas. But it is an important thing for a pilot to remember when he gets separated from his group, or when split up into small units. Also, when actually bouncing a Hun it is good to have as much speed as possible. The aircraft that has speed has the advantage on the one that hasn't. He has the initiative because speed can always be converted into altitude.

The problem of overshooting a Hun comes up quite often in both the P-47 and the P-51 because of the very high overtaking speed they pick up in the dive. And sometimes pilots report after a combat that they couldn't get the Hun they were attacking because they 'overshot him'. And the question is asked, 'How do you avoid overshooting?'

My own idea is that overshooting is a very good thing. Speed is good and should never be lost. When you keep a high speed up you can be sure of closing into range before opening fire, and the closer you get, the better chance you have of hitting him. Also, another good point to remember is that when you are bouncing a Hun you are on the offensive, and have the advantage. But things happen in split seconds up there, and you don't know what might happen, so that you will suddenly find the same Hun, or one of his friends, back on your tail shooting at you. And if you are still going faster than he is, it is easy to pull back on the stick and zoom up above him, where you are ready to attack again.

Capt Duane 'Bee' Beeson, CO of the 334th FS, recounts details of his recently completed escort mission to groundcrewmen (out of shot) at Debden in March 1944. Note the 'Bee' emblem on his flying helmet.

Never give the Hun an even break. If you have any advantage on him, keep it and use it. So, when attacking, I would say plan to overshoot him if possible, and hold fire until within range, then shoot and clobber him down to the last instant before breaking away. It's sorta' like sneaking up behind and hitting him with a baseball bat. When this is done, a pilot will have to be careful not to ram the other aircraft on the breakaway. As he overshoots and pulls up sharply above the Hun, he can take a quick look around to clear his tail, and then concentrate on his Hun again, making as many passes and overshoots as necessary to finish him off.

When the enemy is taking violent evasive action it is hard to get a good shot at him if you are going too fast, so speed can be cut down a little just as long as you are still going faster than he is. An attack of this kind prevents the combat turning into a dogfight with both aircraft at the same speed, each fighting for the advantage. If the Hun sees you coming he can turn into you and meet you semi-head-on, but you can still zoom back up and come down on him again. He can't keep turning circles all day – sooner or later he must break for the deck, and when he does this, he's had it.

Probably the biggest thing to a fighter pilot is being able to see things – not only to see them, but to interpret them. When he sees fighters too far away to recognise, he should have a fairly good idea of whether they are friendly or not by the way they act – by the way they circle a bomber formation or by the way they act when near other fighters that are known to be friendly. This is something that comes pretty much with experience, but a thing that can be practised is just looking and recognising what you see.

The final thing that makes a pilot decide what to do is when he definitely recognises the other aircraft as enemy or friendly – and the farther away it is when he does recognise it, the better chance he'll have to get it, or to avoid boobing if it is a friend.

When flying, it is good to be looking constantly, and you can't look behind too often. Don't look quickly all over the sky – scan it slowly, section by section. When you see something that looks strange, keep an eye on it till it can be identified. The man who gets a Hun is usually the one who has seen it first.

A lot is heard about the use of the sun. It is true that an aircraft attacking out of the sun is very hard to see, which means that, defensively speaking, a pilot should always keep a better look-out in that direction than any other – especially if the sun is anywhere near his own tail. But when bouncing a Hun the sun means very little. When you see a Hun, hit him as fast as possible with everything you have before he gets away. If you wait to position yourself in the sun, the Jerry may be out of reach when you're ready to go. Or someone else may have reached him first and finished him off.

Two of the 4th FG's leading aces pose for an official AAF photograph at Debden in early March 1944. Duane Beeson finished the war with 17.333 aerial victories and 4.75 ground kills and Don Gentile was credited with 21.833 aircraft destroyed in the air and six on the ground. Both men subsequently died in the immediate post-war years, Beeson of a brain tumour in 1947 and Gentile in a flying accident in 1951.

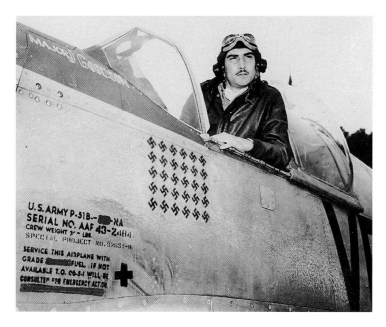

ABOVE: Willard 'Millie' Millikan was flying this P-51B-15 (43-24769) when he was hit by his wingman, 2Lt Sam Young Jr, in P-51B-15 43-24787. The *MISSOURI MAULER* was decorated with 14 victory crosses, although its pilot only claimed 13 kills (he had no probable or damaged credits). Millikan did, however, destroy two aircraft on the ground, so perhaps one of these has been added to his tally. He is seen strapped into the cockpit of the near new fighter at Debden sometime after 22 May 1944, when he had claimed his 13th aerial victory in this very machine. His crew chief, S/Sgt Neal Gallagher, is stood on the wing root.

ABOVE: Another 4th FG ace, Maj James Goodson poses in P-51B 43-24848 VF-B, which features 30 black swastika symbols denoting both his air and ground strafing credits.

The group's famous CO, Donald S Blakeslee, claimed eight and one shared aerial victories while flying Mustangs. These were added to his previous scores of three kills on Thunderbolts and an identical number with the RAF in Spitfires. Blakeslee's assigned Mustangs used in these successes were 43-6437 WD-C and 42-106726 WD-C.

The remaining pilots who shot down five or more enemy aircraft while flying Mustangs with the 4th FG were:

Charles F Anderson   8 and 1 shared air, 5 and 1 shared ground. 5 enemy aircraft in 43-7181 WD-L (Killed in Action 19/4/44)

Bernard L McGrattan 7 and 1 shared air. P-51Bs 43-6767 WD-D and 42-106576 WD-D (Killed in Action 6/6/44)

Pierce W McKennon 7 and 1 shared air, 9 and 3 shared ground. 5 enemy aircraft with P-51B 43-6896 WD-A. Other assigned aircraft P-51B 42-106911 and P-51Ds 44-13883, 44-63166, 44-14221 and 44-72308, all WD-A, and the last four named *RIDGE RUNNER*

ABOVE: As mentioned in the caption above, Willard 'Millie' Millikan also fell victim to a P-51 over Germany, his aircraft being hit by a Mustang whose pilot was attempting to avoid a flak burst over Wittenburg on 30 May 1944. The 13-kill ace became a PoW.

RIGHT: 4th FG ace Pierce McKennon flew a number of Mustangs named *RIDGE RUNNER*. When P-51D 44-14221 WD-A cracked up landing on 17 April 1945, the nose panels with the insignia were simply removed and fitted to the ace's replacement Mustang. The bars on the wing are sighting lines for commencing a dive on a ground target.

Joseph L Lang	7 and 2 shared air. Known P-51Ds 44-13352 QP-Z and 44-14123 QP-Z (Killed in Action 14/10/44)
Albert L Schlegel	7 air and 5 ground. P-51Bs 43-6770 WD-O and 42-106464 WD-O, and P-51D 44-14066 WD-O (Killed in Action 28/8/44)
James A Clark	6 air, 4 and 1 shared ground. P-51Bs 43-6726 QP-W, 43-6560 QP-W and 42-106650 QP-W
Paul S Riley	5 and 2 shared air, 3 ground. P-51B 43-6922 WD-Y (PoW 24/4/44)
Duane W Beeson	5 and 1 shared air, 4 ground. P-51B 43-6819 QP-B *Bee* (PoW 5/4/44)
Van E Chandler	5 air and 4 ground. P-51D 44-14388 VF-U *Wheezy*
Sidney S Woods	5 air (all in one day) P-51D 44-72251 QP-A
David W Howe	5 air. P-51B QP-C and P-51D 44-13884 QP-G
Frank C Jones	5 air. P-51B 43-6897 WD-P and P-51D 44-13389 WD-P
Kendall E Carlson	4 and 2 shared air. P-51B 43-6507 VF-E (PoW 25/2/45)

COMBAT REPORT

CAPTAIN LOUIS H NORLEY

355th FS/4th FG

2 November 1944

Time: 1215 hours

Location: south-east of Leipzig

Conditions: 4 to 6/10ths clouds at 7,000 ft, 10/10ths at 5,000 ft

Our group had rendezvoused with the bombers and were sweeping south of the target under an overcast base at 25,000 ft. At 1410 hrs we saw a large contrail coming up at a steep angle very rapidly east of the target, heading in a westerly direction. Capt Glover, who was leading the group, started after it and managed to keep it in sight from take-off until it made an attack on the bombers and started down again. During this time approximately 11 more of these contrails came up, all headed in the general direction of the bombers. Capt Glover closed on the one he was keeping in sight and recognised it as an Me 163 – he suggested that we stay below the haze in order to catch them on their descent.

I was leading Caboose squadron (in P-51D 44-15028) at 25,000 ft under the layer of haze south-east of the target. We were just completing a port orbit waiting for the jets to come down when one did pop out at 'six o'clock' to me. I immediately dropped my tanks, advancing full boost and revs. I set my gyro sight for 30 ft and closed the graticule to maximum range. I encountered no difficulty in putting the dot on the jet. However, I was quite a little out of range – about 1,000 yards. I got on the jet's tail and followed him down. The jet started pulling away from me, so I fired a few short bursts hoping to make him turn, whereby I could possibly cut him off and get in range. The jet did start to level out and make a port turn – his speed dropped off considerably as his turn increased. I closed on him very rapidly.

I was using a K-14 sight for the first time and do not remember opening the graticule as I closed in. However, I did get a couple of strikes on his tail, firing from 280 yards to 50 yards, ten degrees off. My speed was approximately 450 mph when I got into range. I throttled back but was unable to stay in the turn with him due to my excessive speed. I overshot him, pulled up and got on his tail again.

Up to this time the jet had not been using his blower, at least he was not emitting any black smoke. As I closed on him the second time he used his blower for a couple of seconds and then cut it off again. I closed to 400 yards from 20 degrees off, fired again and saw strikes on his tail. The jet rolled over and started straight down from 8,000 ft with fire coming intermittently from his port side and exhaust. He crashed in a small village and exploded.

Ammunition expended: 450 rounds.

Louis H 'Red Dog' Norley had the unique distinction of serving with all three squadrons within the 4th FG during his two tours in the ETO. He claimed 7.333 kills with the 336th FS (flying P-47s and then P-51s) in his first tour, two more victories whilst serving with the 335th FS at the start of his second spell in the frontline, and then a further pair (although he was only officially credited with one victory) following his move to the 334th FS in January 1945. Norley also commanded both the 334th and 335th FSs at various times between late August 1944 and late September 1945.

20th FG

Of the three pilots who shot down five or more enemy aircraft while flying Mustangs with the 20th FG, the most successful was Ernest C Fiebelkorn, who claimed eight of his nine victories in a P-51. He had at least two Mustangs, the last being P-51D 44-11161 LC-N named *June Nite*. Fiebelkorn, who served with the 77th FS, also claimed two ground victories. He subsequently lost his life in an air accident flying in Korea in 1950.

The remaining two Mustang aces of the 20th were Harley L Brown, with six air and one ground credit, claiming two of his victories flying P-51D 44-11205 KI-A, and Charles H Cole, with five air and six ground victories. The latter pilot started off in the 77th FS with P-51D 44-11324 LC-U, before transferring to the 55th FS and being assigned 44-72160 KI-K. He was shot down in this Mustang and taken prisoner on 25 February 1945.

55th FG

The 20th and 55th FGs converted from P-38 Lightnings at around the same time in the summer of 1944, but the latter group was to be much more successful with the Mustang. The 55th's top-scorer was group CO Elwyn G Righetti, who had seven and one shared aerial victories. His 27 enemy aircraft destroyed by ground-strafing was a record number for any one fighter pilot. Three of Righetti's aerial kills were 'piggyback' Fw 190/Ju 88 *Mistel* combinations. Both his first (P-51D 44-14223 CL-M) and second (P-51D 44-72227 CL-M) Mustangs were named *Katydid*. Righetti was shot down on 17 April 1945 (the date of his 30th birthday) in the second while strafing, and although he was seen to get out of the Mustang, he disappeared and is believed to have been murdered by angry German civilians.

COMBAT REPORT

1st LIEUTENANT ROBERT E WELCH
343rd FS/55th FG
6 February 1945
Time: 1200-1550 hours
Location: Leipzig to Chateauroux
Conditions: heavy overcast, rain and snow

I was leading Red Flight in Tudor squadron on an escort mission to Leipzig. Weather was briefed as being bad, with very strong winds from approximately 345 degrees. Just after target time both my drop tanks went dry, necessitating my heading out sooner than expected. I called Tudor Leader and informed him that I was low on gas and was heading out. He acknowledged my message and informed me to work my way out under the bomber stream. About five minutes later my Number Four man called and said that he was low on oxygen and would have to go to a lower altitude. We dropped down to about 8,000 ft and held a 270-degree heading.

There were many breaks and some areas were clear for 20 miles. We saw a train and proceeded to strafe it. My Number Three man was hit by ground fire and pulled up with his wingman and headed out. I was unable to make contact with Number Three or Four, so I proceeded in a 270-degree heading, strafing targets of opportunity, which consisted of four more trains, not altering our course to search for other targets. Our last target was a train in the south-western part of the Ruhr valley. We then climbed to 6,000 ft and headed for Brussels.

We ran into weather at about 1330 hrs and tried to climb over it to get a fix. We reached 12,000 ft and were still on instruments, and had snow and ice on the windshield. During this time my wingman had called 'Ripsaw', that being the only station to answer after many attempts to contact other stations on B, C and D channels. He received a grid coordinate being of no use to me except to locate my approximate position, which I knew as being west of the Ruhr about 60 miles. We let back down, deciding to look for an airfield by visual means. We flew west for approximately ten minutes and turned south to 200 degrees in order to get into friendly territory.

The weather was very bad, with light rain and snow, cloud bases between 70 ft and 100 ft and visibility about one half-mile. We took up a search for an airfield and called alternate stations continuously. We circled a truck to see if it was Allied or German and my wingman became lost in cloud. We couldn't establish visual contact with each other but agreed to continue our course and search for a field. After an hour's search in friendly territory, I found a field near Chateauroux and landed with approximately 15 gallons of gas. My wingman continued his search, having more gas, and finally landed approximately an hour later with five gallons of fuel at 1550.

My Number Three and Four men, who had started out earlier than my wingman and myself, ran into the same weather and situation. They could not make contact with any stations or locate an airfield by visual means due to weather conditions and bad luck. After trying for two and a half hours they attempted to land wheels down in a wheat field and nosed up both aircraft. Number Three man landed because of battle damage and a lack of gas and Number Four man because of a lack of gas.

William H Lewis was credited with seven aerial victories, five of them trainers caught near Goppingen on 5 September 1944. His assigned P-51D was 44-13907 CY-S. Donald M Cummings had six and a shared in the air, two of which were Me 262s. He had claimed his first kill – a Ju 52/3m – while flying an A-36A with the 27th Fighter Bomb Group in the Mediterranean Theatre of Operations, prior to joining the 38th FS in Britain. His assigned P-51D was 44-15192 CG-U *My Kitten*.

Robert E Welch was credited with six air and 12 ground victories. His first assigned P-51D was 44-14140 CY-O, called *Wings of the Morning*. At the end of March 1945 he changed to 44-72138 CY-Z. Welch was killed in a post-war accident while flying an F-84 Thunderjet.

Bernard H Howes had six aerial victories, three of which were *Mistel* Fw 190/Ju 88 components. He also had two strafing credits. On 3 March 1945 Howes attempted to rescue a downed compatriot in Germany but crashed his P-51D 44-63745 CY-C *Lil' Honey* on take-off and was taken prisoner.

The other 55th FG Mustang aces were:

Dudley M Amos	5 and 1 shared air, 1 and 1 shared ground. P-51D 44-15123 CG-Z (PoW 21/3/45)
William H Allen,	5 air (all trainers on 5/9/44). P-51D 44-14049 CY-J *Pretty Patty II*
Merle M Coons	5 air. P-51D 44-14068 CG-C *The Worry Bird*
Russell C Haworth	4 and 2 shared air. P-51D 44-13642 CL-K *Krazy Kid*
Darrell S Cramer	5 and 2 shared air, 2 ground. P-51D 44-14121 CL-Z *Mick #5*. Cramer had previously shared in shooting down a Japanese bomber while serving with the 339th FS in the South West Pacific Area (SWPA)

ABOVE AND RIGHT: These photographs of John Landers' 44-72218 WZ-I display two forms of personal decoration. The earliest shows six Japanese destroyed symbols and 14 German. The second (right) has six Japanese and 31 faint swastikas. The latter photograph also shows a lighter anti-glare panel bordered with red, as well as a promotion on the canopy frame.

78th FG

The 78th FG may not have produced a Mustang pilot with the necessary five aerial victories to be rated an ace, but its last wartime CO came very close to achieving this feat. John D Landers claimed four and one shared kills flying Mustangs, the first while with the 357th FG. Landers had previously flown P-38s with the 55th FG, and before that P-40s in the SWPA. His total wartime victories amounted to 14 and one shared aerial kills.

339th FG

Of the ten 339th FG pilots that were rated as aces, the highest scorer was Francis R Gerard with eight enemy aircraft shot down. Initially flying P-51B 42-106907 D7-U, his two assigned P-51Ds were 44-13808 D7-U and 44-15003 D7-U, both of which were named *Yi-Yi* after his girlfriend. Gerard brought down five enemy fighters whilst flying the first of these Mustangs.

The other 339th FG aces were:

William E Bryan	7 and 1 shared air, 2 ground. P-51B 42-106798 D7-J and P-51Ds 44-13601 D7-J and 44-15074 D7-J *Big Noise*
Donald A Larson	6 air and 3 ground. P-51D 44-13609 6N-B *Mary Queen of Scots* (Killed in Action 4/8/44)
Robert H Ammon	5 air and 9 ground. P-51D 44-14004 D7-A *Annie Mae*
Christopher J Hanseman	5 air and 2 ground. P-51D 44-13556 6N-H *Eleanor IV* (Killed in Action 29/7/44)
Lester C Marsh	5 air. P-51D 44-14947 D7-P (four of his victories with this aircraft)
Edward H Beavers	5 air. P-51Ds 44-13980 D7-Z and 44-14525 D7-Z *Joanie* (Killed in Action 27/11/44)
Evan M Johnson	5 air. P-51Ds 44-13471 6N-J *The Comet* and 44-15039 6N-J *Pistol Packin' Mama*
Jack S Daniell	5 air (all Fw 190s in one mission). P-51D 44-14734 6N-K *Sweet'n Low Down* (left side) and *Sweet and Lowdown* (right side)
James R Starnes	4 and 4 shared air, 6 ground. P-51B 42-106936 6N-X and P-51Ds 44-14113 6N-X, 44-14387 6N-X and 44-72152 6N-X, all called *Tar Heel*

Christopher J Hanseman, mentioned above, was a few days short of his 20th birthday when he was shot down while strafing. Frank Olynyk, the US fighter pilot scores authority, finds Hanseman the youngest American ace of the war.

352nd FG

The 352nd FG's 22 Mustang aces were headed by George E Preddy with 22 and four shared aerial victories and five by strafing. Preddy was the most successful Mustang pilot of the Eighth Air Force. He also scored three kills while flying P-47s. Preddy claimed five aircraft shot down and two shared destroyed while flying his first assigned P-51B 42-106451 HO-P *Cripes A'Mighty*. A further 15 and two shared claimed were then made in replacement P-51D 44-13321 HO-P *Cripes A'Mighty 3rd*, including a record six Bf 109s on the mission of 6 August 1944.

Like most of the great Mustang aces in the ETO, George Preddy was regularly photographed by both the USAAF and the press.

COMBAT REPORT

MAJOR GEORGE E PREDDY
487th FS/352nd FG
12 June 1944
Time: 1025-1035 hours
Location: south-west of Rennes
Conditions: 4/10ths cumulus cloud at 8,000 ft

I was leading the group (in P-51B 42-106451 HO-P) that was giving area support to bombers attacking various targets in the vicinity of Rennes. A group of about 18 B-24s were last out and withdrawing in the vicinity of Rennes when 12 Me 109s made a quarter stern attack on them from out of the sun. We headed for them on the same level and some turned into us, with others breaking for the deck. I followed one down, firing from various ranges and angles. I got a few hits and the enemy aircraft lost most of its speed, causing me to overshoot. I pulled above him and was starting another attack when the pilot baled out at 8,000 ft. I claim one Me 109 destroyed.

Ammunition expended: 835 rounds.

COMBAT ANALYSIS

MAJOR GEORGE E PREDDY
487th FS/352nd FG
May 1944

It is an old story that the pilot who doesn't get across the Channel will not see any action. One of the big problems in this theatre is weather, and since a good 50 per cent of our flying is done in instrument conditions, it is necessary that all pilots be proficient at instrument and close formation flying. The formation used going through an overcast is as follows. In the flight, the number two man flies on the leader's left wing, with three and four on the right. In the squadron the flights fly line astern, stacked down. The whole outfit is in very close, and if each man flies a steady position, it is possible to take 16 or 20 ships through an overcast. If visibility in the soup is very bad or turbulence exists, it becomes necessary to split the squadron into sections of two or more.

On the climb out, the flights and individual ships fly close formation, as this reduces throttle jockeying and saves gas. When we approach the enemy coast, everybody moves out into battle formation – i.e. line abreast and five or six ships' lengths apart for individual ships and line abreast for each two flights. This is an easy formation to fly when flying a straight course, and offers excellent cross cover.

When escorting several large boxes of bombers it is impossible to keep the group together, so squadrons and sections of squadrons are assigned a particular section of the task force. We usually fly two flights of four aeroplanes each together. The flights fly line abreast to offer cross cover, but if the lead ship is turning a lot it is necessary to fall in string. Normally, the flight leaders and element leaders look for bounces, with the wingmen on the defensive. This doesn't mean that leaders never look back or wingmen never look down. It is impossible to see everything, but each pilot must keep his head moving and look to find the enemy.

When a member of the flight sees something suspicious, he calls it in and the leader takes the section to investigate. When it is identified as the enemy, we notice the number and formation and try to make a surprise. The first flight of four goes down and the second flight stays up for top cover. It is necessary to have this protection, as a decent bounce cannot be made when trying to protect your own tail. If only one flight is in the vicinity, the second element acts as top cover. If a surprise can be made on several enemy aircraft, all ships in the flight can pick one out and drive up behind them and shoot them down. If the Hun sees you coming from above he usually starts diving and turning.

It is necessary for the wingman to stay with his leader, as the leader cannot follow the Hun through evasive action and do a good job of shooting unless the wingman is there to guard against attack by another enemy aircraft. Should the attacking flight or element get bounced, the wingman turns into the attack immediately and calls the leader.

When the leader is preparing to make a bounce, he should inform his squadron of his intentions. If a wingman sees an enemy aeroplane which would get away if he doesn't act immediately, he goes down on the bounce, calling in as he does so. In this case the leader becomes the wingman.

When being bounced, the first thing is always turn into the attack. The flight does not follow the leader into the turn, but each ship turns into the attackers.

If a pilot sees an enemy aircraft behind him in firing range he must take evasive action immediately. He slips and skids the ship as much as possible, giving the Hun maximum deflection. It is a good idea to turn in the direction of friendly aeroplanes so they can shoot or scare Jerry off your tail.

There will be times after a combat that you are down on the deck. If you are alone and can't find a friend to join with, the best thing to do is head for home, taking advantage of clouds for cover. If there are two or more they should climb back up providing they still have speed and gas. They should push everything to the firewall and keep speed in the climb – the leader must do a lot of turning in order to keep the men behind him up. Each man must be on the lookout for a bounce and watch each others' tail. If there are only two or three of you, you should find friends and join them.

As a conclusion, when escorting bombers it is a good idea to range out to the sides, front and rear, and hit enemy fighters before they can get to the bomber formation, but do not run off on a wild goose chase and leave the bombers unprotected.

In all groups the policy as to who makes bounces, and under what circumstances, is arranged well beforehand, and is thoroughly understood by all in order to avoid indecision.

George Preddy poses for the camera after his successful action on 6 August 1944 when he shot down six enemy aircraft on one mission. His victory crosses were formed with white outlines directly onto the blue nose marking. The name on 44-13321 HO-P was applied in white and black.

In October 1944 Preddy moved from the 487th to the 328th FS as CO, taking P-51D 44-14906 (which was then coded PE-P and named *Cripes A'Mighty*) with him. He shot down another four enemy fighters with this aircraft prior to meeting his death in it on 25 December 1944. Preddy was shot down in error by a US Army anti-aircraft battery.

John C Meyer, a squadron and group CO, also had an impressive score of 20 and two shared aerial and 13 ground-strafing kills. Meyer, like Preddy, had previously shot down three enemy aircraft with the P-47. Five and a shared victory were obtained while flying P-51B 42-106471 HO-M *Lambie II*, then at least eight and a shared with P-51D 44-15041 HO-M *Petie 3rd*. In between using these two aircraft, Meyer had another assigned P-51D, 44-14151 HO-M *Petie 2nd*, during the summer of 1944 in which he did not obtain any air victories.

William T Whisner was credited with 14 and one shared in P-51s, and also had three strafing victories. His P-51B was 42-106449 HO-W *Princess Elizabeth*, but 12 of his victories were obtained flying P-51D 44-14237 HO-W *Moonbeam McSwine*.

John F Thornell claimed 12 and two shared aerial victories and two ground kills in Mustangs, having previously obtained four and a shared flying Thunderbolts. Eight and the shared victories were scored flying P-51B 42-106872 PE-T *Pattie Ann II*.

RIGHT: 'Ace in a day'. Capt Bill Whisner of the 352nd FG's 487th FS signals his mission haul following a large-scale engagement with 50 plus Fw 190s near Leipzig on 21 November 1944. His claim for six kills was later downgraded to five confirmed and one probable, taking his tally at that time to 9.5 aerial victories. Finishing the war with 15.5 aerial victories (and three strafing kills), Whisner scored 12 of these in P-51D 44-14237 *Moonbeam McSWINE*. He would later claim a further 5.5 MiG-15 victories flying the F-86 Sabre in Korea in 1951-52.

COMBAT REPORT

1ST LIEUTENANT JOHN F THORNELL JR

328th FS/352nd FG

12 June 1944

Time: 1025-1030 hours

Location: south of St Malo

Conditions: Cloud at lower altitudes

I was leading the squadron (in P-51B PE-T 42-106872) on an area support and escort mission for heavy bombers in the area south of St Malo. We rendezvoused with the bombers on time and stayed with them, patrolling the area, until 1025 hrs. At that time I picked up the last two boxes of bombers coming off their target. We were at 21,000 ft. I noticed several aircraft making a bounce on the bombers. I saw a B-24 go down, so I immediately called the squadron to drop their external gas tanks and attack the bandits, which turned out to be ten or twelve Me 109s, with four or five FW 190s as top cover.

I pulled up behind one enemy aircraft and started firing at about 150 yards. I saw a few strikes. He broke for the deck and I followed him. On the deck I closed to about 100 yards and hit the Me 109 in the wing roots and shot about three feet off the end of his right wing. Many pieces were flying back from the enemy aircraft. At this time he caught fire, but I had to pull out as I was being bounced by the FW 190s. Lt McCarthy fired when I pulled up and he also hit the enemy aircraft. At this time the enemy aircraft was flaming fiercely, and it looked as if the enemy pilot was trying to bale out. We climbed into the FW 190s and lost them so we pulled out of the area.

Crossing out at 1050 hrs, we proceeded for home without further incident, except much flak and ground fire at low altitude. I claim one Me 109 destroyed, shared with Lt McCarthy.

Ammunition expended: 652 rounds.

The victory markings on Capt John Thornell's 42-106872 PE-T *PATTIE ANN II* took the form of black and white swastikas superimposed on red discs. Crew names are recorded in black. The 352nd FG's blue nose marking extended right back to the cockpit and covered the standard anti-dazzle olive drab.

LEFT AND BELOW: Two of the high-scoring aces in the 487th FS both had the individual letter M as their personal mark, which was also the initial letter of their surnames. Glennon Moran flew P-51C 42-103320 HO-M and John Meyer P-51D 44-14151 HO-M in the summer of 1944. Moran's M (an earlier aircraft) had the individual letter on both fin and fuselage, whereas Meyer's only had the M on the fin, which became the standard location on 352nd FG aircraft. The blue nose marking followed the panel line at the start of its upward sweep.

The other 352nd FG Mustang aces were:

Glennon T Moran	11 and 2 shared air, 3 ground (one with a P-47). Ten of the victories were obtained with P-51C 42-103320 HO-<u>M</u>
Raymond H Littge	10 and 1 shared air, 13 ground. P-51B 42-103320 HO-<u>M</u> *Silver Dollar* (originally G T Moran's aircraft) and P-51Ds 44-13320 HO-<u>M</u> *E Pluribus Unum* and 44-72216 HO-<u>M</u> *Miss Helen*
William T Halton	9 and 1 shared air (plus one with a P-47), 2 ground. P-51B 42-106717 PE-T and P-51Ds 44-13966 PE-T and 44-14812 HO-T, all with the name *Slender, Tender and Tall*
Donald S Bryan	9 air (3 and 3 shared with P-47s). P-51B 43-6894 PE-B *Little One II* and P-51D 44-14061 PE-B *Little One III* (eight of his victories were in this last aircraft)
Stanford K Moats	8 and 1 shared air. P-51B 42-106751 HO-U *Kay* and P-51D 44-14848 HO-K *Kay III*
Carl J Luksic	8 and 1 shared air, 7 ground. P-51Bs 43-7145 HO-Z, 43-7188 HO-Z (both named *Elly's Lucky Boy*, although name not applied) and 42-106788 HO-Z (PoW 24/5/44)
Charles J Cesky	8 and 1 shared air. P-51Ds 44-13927 PE-L *Diann Ruth* and 44-13401 PE-L *Diann Ruth II*
Henry J Miklajcyk	7 and 1 shared air, 6 ground. P-51B 42-106430 PZ-K *The Syracusan* and P-51D 44-13690 PZ-K *The Syracusan 3rd*
Frank A Cutler	7 and 1 shared air, 3 ground. P-51B 43-6578 PZ-P *Soldier's Vote* (Killed in Action 13/5/44)
Stephen W Andrew	7 air (plus one with a P-47 and one in SWPA). P-51B 42-106467 PZ-A (6 victories with this aircraft) (PoW 2/7/44)
Walter E Starck	6 air (plus one with P-47). P-51B 43-24807 HO-X *Starck Mad* and P-51B 43-6929 HO-X *Starck Mad*
Willie O Jackson	6 air (plus one with a P-47). P-51B 42-106661 PZ-J *Hot Stuff* and P-51Ds 44-13398 PZ-J and 44-14709 PZ-J
Edwin L Heller	5 and 1 shared air, 16.5 ground. P-51B 43-6704 PZ-<u>H</u> and P-51D 44-14696 PZ-<u>H</u>, both named *Hell-er Bust*
Ernest O Bostrom	5 air. P-51D 44-13929 PZ-O *Little Marjie*
Earl R Lazear	5 air. P-51D 44-14877 PZ-L *Pennie's Earl*
Alex F Sears	5 air, 1 ground. P-51D 44-14788 HO-E *The Sheepherder*
Duerr H Schuh	5 air. P-51D 44-13530 HO-A *Duchess*
William J Stangel	4 and 2 shared air. P-51D 44-14015 PE-C *Stinky II*

353rd FG

The most successful pilot with the Mustang in the 353rd FG was Wayne K Blickenstaff. An original combat pilot of the Group, he was able only to make probably destroyed or damage claims during his first tour flying Thunderbolts. During his second tour, commenced in the autumn of 1944, Blickenstaff flew Mustangs and shot down ten enemy aircraft. His assigned P-51D was 44-72374 LH-U *Betty E.*

Arthur C Cundy had claimed six aerial victories during the winter of 1944-45, but then lost his life on 11 March 1945 when his Mustang went down in the North Sea after suffering engine trouble. His assigned P-51D was 44-15092 SX-<u>B</u> *Alabama Rammer Jammer.*

The other 353rd FG P-51 aces were:

Horace Q Waggoner 5 air, 7 and 1 shared ground. P-51K 44-11565 *Miss Illini II* and
P-51D 44-14802 SX-X *Miss Illini III*

Robert A Elder 5 air (all on 24/3/45), 2 ground. P-51D 44-72736 LH-S
Miss Gamble

Gene E Markham 5 air. P-51Ds 44-14949 YJ-Q *Mr Gray* and 44-72171 YJ-Q *Mr Gray II*

355th FG

The top-scoring pilot of the 355th FG in the Mustang was Henry W Brown, who shot down
14 enemy aircraft and shared in another. Brown was also credited with 15 and a share by
ground-strafing. His first victories were obtained flying P-51B 42-106448 WR-Z *Hun
Hunter/Texas*. Its replacement was P-51D 44-13305 WR-Z with the same name, and he
obtained most of his remaining victories with this aircraft. Brown was shot down by flak in this
Mustang on 3 October 1944 and taken prisoner.

ABOVE AND RIGHT: Henry Brown's 355th FG P-51D, with unit-applied dark
green camouflage on the uppersurfaces of wings, tailplane and fuselage decking
– the paint was also taken up the leading edge of the fin. The black C on the
rudder identifies the flight. The name *The HUN HUNTER/TEXAS* had been
added and the victories display grown to a third line by the time the kilted
youngster had his photograph taken while excitedly clasping a hand gun!
Brown was shot down by flak in this aircraft on 3 October 1944.

P-51B-10-NA 42-106448 of the 354th FS/355th FG, Steeple Morden, April 1944
**Perfectly illustrating unit-applied camouflage, this aircraft was the second P-51B assigned to
2Lt Henry W Brown, who used it to shoot down at least three enemy aircraft in March and
April 1944. In June of that year Brown received one of the first P-51Ds (44-13305) issued to
the 355th FG, and 42-106448 was in turn passed on to other pilots. The aircraft endured in
operational service until the end of the year, and was eventually salvaged by the 4th
Strategic Air Depot in February 1945.**

RIGHT: William Hovde named all his assigned fighters after the familiar term for his father, Ole. *OLE-II* was P-51B 43-6928 YF-I, and it was unusual in not only carrying a record of the sorties completed by the pilot in this aircraft (seven when this photograph was taken), but also Hovde's 43 flown in P-47s, all recorded with yellow 'bomb' symbols.

BELOW: The film type used for this photograph of William Hovde's P-51D 44-73155 shows the fighter's yellow nose band and rudder in a deceptively dark shade. The Nazi flag victory symbols were carried right around the canopy of *OLE-VI*. The Russian spelling of Hovde's full name below the exhaust stubs was inspired by his participation in a shuttle flight to the USSR.

BELOW: The 355th FG's Claiborne Kinnard was the first combat commander of the 354th FS, which had a bulldog for its emblem, hence *The Bulldogs* and the number 1 titling on the engine cowling – the latter signified that this Mustang was the CO's mount. All of Kinnard's P-51s were named *MAN O'WAR*, painted in white on an irregular shaped red backing. This particular P-51B is 43-6431 WR-A, which has had its fin and rudder type identity bands painted out. Note that the aircraft also boasts a highly sought after 'blown' Malcolm hood.

No other 355th FG pilot ran a score into double figures with Mustangs, although William J Hovde came close with nine and a share and also two strafing victories. He had previously shot down an enemy aircraft while flying a P-47, and in the Korean War he was credited with a MiG. All Hovde's aircraft were given his father's nickname. Machines known to have been assigned to him included P-51B 43-6928 *Ole II* and P-51Ds 44-13531 *Ole III*, 44-14541 *Ole IV*, 44-73155 *Ole VI*.

The remaining 15 P-51 aerial aces of this group were:

Claiborne H Kinnard 8 air (one with 4th FG), 17 ground. P-51B 43-6431 WR-A and
                     P-51Ds 44-13375 WR-A, 44-15625 WR-A and 44-73144 WR-A,
                     all named *Man O'War*

BELOW: Claiborne Kinnard's third *MAN O'WAR* was yet another 354th FS Mustang with 'in-the-field' camouflage on the fuselage confined to the top decking. Like Kinnard's previous fighters with this name, it was painted in white on a red bulged shape backing.

John L Elder	7 air (plus one with a P-47), 13 ground. P-51B 42-106733 OS-R *Moon*, and P-51Ds 44-63633 OS-R and 44-73065 OS-R
Gordon M Graham	7 air, 9 and 1 shared ground. P-51Ds 44-14275 WR-F *Down For Double* and P-51D 44-15255 WR-F
Bert W Marshall	7 air and 3 ground. P-51Ds 44-14293 WR-B *Jane II*, 44-14409 WR-<u>B</u> *Jane III*, 44-14799 WR-B *Jane IV*, 44-15279 WR-B, 44-72253 WR-B *Jane VI* and 44-72953 WR-<u>B</u> *Jane VII*
Everett W Stewart	7 air (plus 1.5 in P-47s with 352nd FG) and 1 and 1 shared ground. P-51Ds 44-13540 WR-<u>S</u> *Sunny VI* and 44-15255 WR-<u>S</u> *Sunny VII*
Robert E Woody	6 and 4 shared air, 2 ground. P-51B 43-6520 WR-W *Woody's Maytag*
Fred R Haviland	6 air and 6 ground. P-51D 44-14402 OS-H *Barbara*
Henry S Bille	6 air and 4 ground. P-51B 42-106634 OS-K and P-51Ds 44-13945 OS-K, 44-14314 OS-K and 44-72311 OS-K, all of which were named *Prune Face*
Leslie D Minchew	5 and 1 shared air. P-51B 43-7103 OS-O and P-51D 44-14753 OS-<u>O</u>

ABOVE: Capt Robert Woody's 43-6520 WR-R was marked with simple white swastikas applied onto the fighter's Olive Drab camouflage. Woody was one of the most successful 355th FG pilots in the early days. In this posed shot, taken after he had destroyed 4.5 Bf 109s on 24 April 1944, one of the groundcrew mechanics is making sure he is clear of the pilot's name, recorded in yellow just forward of the windshield.

ABOVE: A blue rudder and nose band identified 357th FS aircraft within the 355th FG. P-51D 44-72311 OS-K was the last of Henry Bille's personal Mustangs. Named *Prune Face* on the left side of the nose, it carried *EDIE* on the right in black.

LEFT: Most fighters had the assigned pilot's name and that of the groundcrew painted on the aircraft. They were confined to pilot and crew chief only on P-51D 44-14753 OS-<u>O</u>, flown by ace Les Minchew.

William J Cullerton	5 air and 15 ground. P-51Ds 44-13677 OS-X *Miss Steve* and 44-64011 OS-X (PoW 8/4/45)
James N McElroy	5 air and 6 ground. P-51B 43-7023 YF-S *Big Stoop* and P-51D 44-14498 YF-S *Big Stoop II*
Norman S Fortier	5 air and 5 and 1 shared ground. Most with P-51B 42-106870 WR-N, and also flew P-51Ds 44-15373 WR-N and 44-72361 WR-N
Charles D Hauver	5 air. P-51Ds 44-14090 WR-R *Princess Pat* and 44-14704 WR-R *Princess Pat II* (all kills with this latter aircraft)
Royce W Priest	5 air. P-51Ds 44-13764 WR-E and 44-15652 WR-E
Charles W Lenfest	4 air and 3 shared, 2 and 1 shared ground. P-51Bs 43-6948 WR-F *Lorie II* and 42-106874 WR-F *Lorie III* and P-51D 44-14275 WR-F *Lorie IV* (PoW 3/10/44)

ABOVE AND RIGHT: Strafing ace William Cullerton's 44-13677 OS-X *MISS STEVE* displaying 18 of his credited 20 air and ground kills. Later the victim of a crash-landing, the aircraft did not suffer serious damage and was repaired. Cullerton was shot down in another aircraft on 8 April 1945.

356th FG

The 356th FG's fortunes in air combat improved greatly with its conversion to the P-51. Of the three pilots who shot down five or more enemy aircraft with the Mustang, the leading ace was Donald J Strait, who had ten and one shared destroyed. He had previously claimed three aerial kills while flying Thunderbolts. Most of his P-51 victories were obtained in P-51D 44-15152 QI-T *JERSEY JERK*.

The remaining two aces both scored five aerial victories each, with Clinton D Burdick also sharing in the shooting down of a sixth enemy aircraft, as well as claiming a strafing credit. His P-51D was 44-15310 QI-B *Do Do*. Wilbur R Scheible scored five aerial victories in Mustangs and one in a P-47, and was also credited with three strafing kills in the Mustang. His P-51D was 44-15083 QI-Z.

Maj Don Strait leads his squadron during an escort mission to the oil refinery near Lützkendorf on 9 February 1945. On this day the 356th FG helped escort 304 heavy bombers from the 1st Air Division. Only one 303rd BG B-17 was lost through enemy action, and the escorts made no claims. Five days later Don Strait destroyed two German fighters with this very machine south of Chemnitz.

P-51D-15-NA 44-15152 of the 361st FS/356th FG, Martlesham Heath, February 1945
This colourful aircraft was used from November 1944 through to May 1945 by ranking group ace, and CO of the 361st FS, Donald Strait. It is known that at least six (and possibly as many as 10.5) victories were achieved by Strait in 44-15152, which was named for his home state of New Jersey. Remaining with the 356th FG until VE-Day, the spinner of this aircraft was later painted all blue.

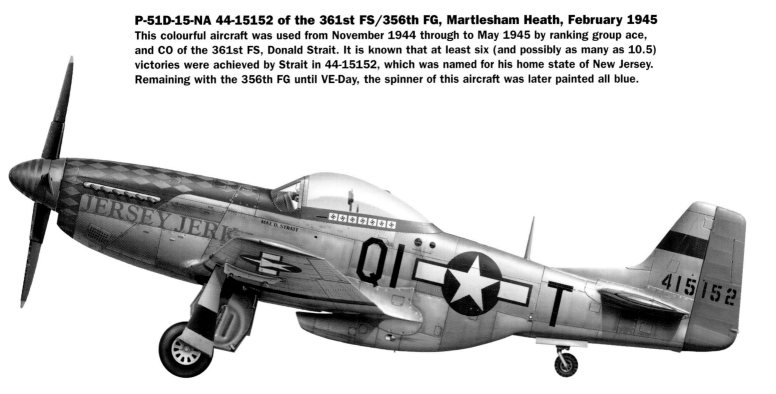

COMBAT ANALYSIS

Lieutenant Colonel Everett W Stewart
Executive Officer (Flying) 355th FG
April 1944

Individual Combat

In individual combat with P-51 aircraft against fighters, it is essential to move in quickly to firing range within the rapid acceleration of the P-51. If an enemy aircraft gets into a good dive before one can get into range, difficulty is usually encountered in closing. The P-51 and Me 109 seem to be about on par for dive and low altitude speed. The P-51 will out-turn the Me 109 at any altitude up to 25,000 ft (performance above that altitude is unknown). Greater difficulty is encountered in out-turning the Fw 190.

I believe that steep, uncoordinated turning is the best evasive action for the P-51 if the enemy aircraft is within firing range. When the turn is then tightened, an average pilot should be able to come into deflection shooting range of enemy aircraft by using a smooth, steep turn. Then, if the enemy aircraft elects to dive away the P-51 should be able to get astern of him. Luckily, I haven't had to use any violent evasive action as yet.

'Ev' Stewart was one of only a handful of pilots to serve command postings with three fighter groups in the ETO. CO of the 352nd FG's 328th FS upon the group's arrival in England, he was posted to the 355th FG as its Executive Officer in January 1944. Made CO of the Steeple Morden-based group ten months later, Stewart was subsequently sent to lead the 4th FG in February 1945. Prior to his time in the ETO, he had already completed a tour of duty in the Pacific – which included being at Pearl Harbor on 7 December 1941! All of this frontline flying meant that 'Ev' Stewart participated in no less than 180 missions, totalling 510 hours of 'stick time', during the Second World War.

Two-Ship Element

In attacking with two ships, I like for my wingman to drop back to a position about 250 to 300 yards out to either side, and about 250 to 300 yards to the rear, in such a position where he can completely cover the two of us from attack. I do not like for the wingman to be trying to shoot one down while I am shooting unless, of course, we are in some so-called 'perfect' set-up. I prefer to give him the next victory and let me cover. My wingmen nearly always get to fire if I fire, and they usually come home with a victory.

Defensively, I like to have him fly as nearly line abreast as he can maintain. If the enemy aircraft actually attack, we break sharply into the attack and up, if possible. If we can thus get the advantage we can become offensive. If not, we just have to fight. If it is possible to get up into sun, the Hun will usually lose you, or keep going down.

Four-Ship Flight

The four-ship flight is held together just as long as possible, both offensively and defensively. The Hun definitely respects four-ships which will work together, and usually will not attack until he sees he has every other advantage, plus numbers of two or three to one. In attacking with four-ships, the flight leader and the element leader move in to fire with the wingmen covering. Wingmen should stay with the leader until both have to split into a life and death dogfight. In flights deep into Germany, wingmen usually get their fighting and firing.

General Information

1. From enemy coast to rendezvous, I like to keep the squadrons fairly compact in a close line abreast battle formation. This adds to better manoeuvring between and around flak areas, and prevents straggling flights and individuals. It is easier to fly than wide spread formations, and still affords pilots ample opportunity to look around.

2. Upon rendezvousing with bombers, I usually take the lead squadron over the lead portion of the bombers, with one section of eight on each side. Another squadron is despatched to the rear bomber units in the same manner, and both perform close escort. The top cover squadron is placed 2,000 to 4,000 ft above the bombers to watch the approach of enemy aircraft from above and far out. If an extremely large force is to be covered by one group, the third squadron is then placed fairly close in on the centre section of the bombers..

3. In recent escort missions, flights and sections have quite frequently had to work independently along bombers, and use their own judgement on when to attack. They give a call if they have to leave for a bounce, or are bounced, and someone else is sent or moves into their area if possible.

4. Squadron and flight leaders will usually make the bounces until they get at least one victory, then we like to pass it around. If any leader fails to see a 'called in' aircraft, however, he will immediately despatch the individual who spots it after the enemy aircraft and give him cover.

5. If two flights can remain together on escort they will usually fly 500 to 1000 yards apart.

6. Flights use line abreast, with about 300 yards between individuals.

7. We find it quite difficult to get the squadrons back together after combat in recent encounters, as the Germans usually hit in large numbers, and there is plenty of combat and chasing to keep everyone busy.

8. On deep penetrations there is no need to scatter flights all over the sky. The Germans hit in large numbers at one portion of the bombers if they come up at all, and the more flights that can be kept close in to the bombers for call, the more people we can actually get into the initial fight.

Defensive

1. When enemy aircraft are in a position to attack, and we are free to fight, we try to climb up to enemy aircraft and engage. As long as we can see the enemy aircraft, we do not feel that we are at a disadvantage.

2. From recent experience, the size of the enemy's aircraft formation has not much influenced our response, except when it numbers less than 20, then we might send only one squadron in to attack or break up the attack. The more enemy aircraft in the formation, the more we can shoot down.

3. On penetration and before rendezvous, enemy aircraft may start attacking before tanks are dropped. If possible, a small force will be despatched to break up enemy aircraft so others may continue to rendezvous. After rendezvous, we usually drop tanks when enemy aircraft get in the immediate vicinity. Tanks are always kept as long as possible.

4. Radio transmission is used to designate assembly point for the group after a combat. We usually try to assemble over a certain part of the bomber formation.

5. We usually stay and fight with enemy aircraft, and hit the deck only when chasing enemy aircraft. If possible, it is always best to come out of enemy territory at above 15,000 ft.

Offensive

1. If I am in a favourable position I will usually take the first bounce myself. After that I will despatch any flight or element out that spots enemy aircraft. A rule of thumb cannot be set down for bouncing, as conditions right at that instant will govern just how you proceed with your attack.

2. I like to send about the same number down as there are enemy aircraft, with a flight or more as cover.

3. Our tactic when an enemy aircraft has the advantage is to usually head right for him and start a fight. We are usually able to stay together longer for teamwork than the Hun, and he will soon lose his advantage.

4. We try to keep one squadron with the bombers – and thus enable squadrons chasing enemy aircraft to stay with them until they are destroyed or widely dispersed – when they strike in forces of about 50 or more. Usually, they will not strike with less than 50, and we seldom, if ever, find more than one such formation.

5. Every effort is made to engage enemy aircraft before they can get to the bombers. If they can be caught then, it is easier to get more of them as they are concentrating on the bombers and become more confused when attacked.

6. By making our presence immediately known to the Hun, we can sometimes avert their attack entirely. And if he does indeed attack, it will usually be a feeble attack, giving us plenty of opportunity to pursue him.

7. While our formation is together the flight and element leaders may start a bounce, provided they call it in. If the leader does not desire them to continue the bounce or leave formation, they are immediately recalled. When we are with the bombers their liberty is extended.

RIGHT: This photograph, taken in August 1944, shows the assigned aircraft (left to right) of pilots Edwin Hiro, Donald Bochkay, William O'Brien and Robert Foy. They are 44-13518 B6-D (missing with Hiro on 19 September 1944), 44-13681 B6-F, 44-13522 B6-G *Billy's Bitch* (missing in action on 17 August 1944 with another pilot) and 44-13712 B6-V *RELUCTANT REBEL* (missing in action on 10 August 1944 with another pilot). Most P-51Ds of the 363rd FS were camouflaged soon after their arrival at Leiston – dark green upper and light grey undersurfaces. Code letters were either reinstated on the D-Day stripes in black or the B6 was repainted further forward on the fuselage.

357th FG

Leonard K Carson headed the list of 42 pilots who 'made ace' with the Mustang whilst serving with the 357th FG. During two tours with the 362nd FS Carson shot down 18 enemy aircraft and shared in the destruction of another. He was also credited with destroying three and one shared by strafing. His assigned Mustangs were P-51B 43-6634 G4-C *Nooky Booky*, P-51Ds 44-13316 G4-C *Nooky Booky II* and 44-14896 G4-C *Nooky Booky III* and P-51K 44-11622 G4-C *Nooky Booky IV*.

Next came John B England with 16 and three shared in the air. His assigned aircraft were P-51B 42-106462 G4-H *U'VE HAD IT!* and P-51Ds 44-13735 G4-H *U'VE HAD IT!* and 44-14789 G4-E *MISSOURI ARMADA*. England lost his life in a crash in France on 17 November 1954.

LEFT: *U'VE HAD IT!* was a commonly heard British wartime expression that was adopted by John England as the name for his P-51B 42-106462 G4-H, which is seen here in June 1944. The name was applied in red. Mission symbols, which included three ducks for recalls, were painted in yellow on the olive drab. The victory symbols were applied in black directly onto the bare metal. Unusually, the cross indicating the fitting of the fuselage fuel tank was painted in white on the bare metal.

ABOVE AND RIGHT: The 357th FG produced more pilots with ace status than any other Eighth Air Force Mustang group. Highest scorer was Leonard Carson with 18 and one shared aerial victories. His last Mustang was P-51K 44-11622 G4-C *Nooky Booky IV*. The name was applied in red, with yellow highlights. Its canopy inscription was *MAJ. KIT CARSON*, Kit being his nickname. The forward end of the top line of victories was for Carson's ground strafing credits.

RIGHT: John England's fourth assigned Mustang was 44-14789 G4-E, nicknamed *MISSOURI ARMADA*. It was one of the 362nd FS aircraft given a complete 'in-the-field' camouflage scheme in the late summer of 1944, as this photo clearly shows.

RIGHT: Richard Peterson's P-51D 44-14868 was the last of his three fighters named *HURRY HOME HONEY*, all of which were coded C5-T. Its name is believed to have been painted in blue.

BELOW LEFT AND RIGHT: Two of the aircraft seen in the 363rd FS formation photograph on page 84 are shown individually in these two shots. Both displaying their uppersurfaces, each Mustang is clearly marked with white type identity bands on the wings and tailplanes. Don Bochkay's winged motif can be seen on the engine compartment of B6-F, and likewise a girlie painting on Foy's B6-V *Reluctant Rebel*. Bochkay applied no name to this P-51D, or the final two assigned Mustangs he flew in the ETO.

RIGHT: Clarence 'Bud' Anderson's fighters were all named *OLD CROW* and coded B6-S. The last was 44-14450, which sports 17 victory symbols for 16 air and one ground strafing credit. The name was painted in white. This aircraft wore standard green and grey camouflage for much of Anderson's second tour (which ran from September 1944 through to January 1945), the paint being stripped off by the fighter's groundcrew in November 1944.

RIGHT: Donald Bochkay's penultimate Mustang touches down on 10 December 1945. The small Nazi flag victory symbols are visible just below the windshield frame. Two of Bochkay's victories were obtained in this aircraft, which was written-off in an accident in January 1945.

RIGHT AND BELOW: Two views of Don Bochkay's last P-51D (44-72244), with his distinctive winged ace of clubs motif. That these photographs were taken post-VE-Day is evidenced by the squadron code painted under the left wing.

COMBAT REPORT

2nd LIEUTENANT MORRIS A STANLEY
364th FS/357th FG
6 March 1944
Time: 1410 hours
Location: Brandenburg, Germany
Conditions: 6 to 8/10ths cloud

I was Gowdy White Four in the element led by Flt Off McKinney. We sighted three Me 110s in the vicinity and immediately attacked. I pulled up dead astern to the aircraft on the left. At 250 yards I opened fire, observing strikes on the left wing, left engine nacelle and cockpit. I closed to 100 yards and gave him another burst, observing strikes on the right engine nacelle. At this time both engines started to smoke badly and then burst into flames. Sections of the right wing and canopy flew off. As I ceased firing and pulled off to one side, I saw the flaming Me 110 reel on its back and start a slow spiral to the right, apparently out of control.

The last time I saw the enemy aircraft it was spinning violently earthwards covered from one engine to the other in flames and smoke. No evasive action was taken by the enemy aircraft at any time during combat. No firing was seen from the rear gun position of the enemy aircraft at any time. I claim one Me 110 destroyed.

Ammunition expended: 160 rounds.

Another pilot with 16 aerial victories, plus one shared, was Clarence E 'Bud' Anderson, who also had a strafing credit. His aircraft were P-51Bs 43-6723 B6-S, 43-12454 B6-S and 43-24823 B6-S and P-51D 44-14450 B6-S, all named *OLD CROW*.

Robert W Foy had 15 aerial and three ground victories. Two of his assigned P-51Ds were 44-13712 B6-V *Reluctant Rebel* and 44-63621 B6-V *Little Shrimp*. Foy was killed in a flying accident in 1950.

Richard A Peterson had 14 and three shared aerial credits and three and one shared strafing kills. His assigned aircraft, P-51B 43-6935 C5-T and P-51Ds 44-13586 C5-T and P-51D 44-14868 C5-T, were all named *Hurry Home Honey*.

Donald H Bochkay had 13 and two shared aerial victories. His aircraft were P-51C 42-103041 B6-F *Speedball Alice*, P-51B 43-6963 B6-F *Alice In Wonderland* and P-51Ds 44-13681 B6-F, 44-15422 B6-F and 44-72244 B6-F.

Two other pilots ran their scores into double figures, namely John A Kirla with 11 and one shared aerial kills in P-51Ds 44-14625 G4-H *SPOOK* and 44-72180 G4-H *SPOOK*, and Charles E 'Chuck' Yeager, who also had 11 and one shared in the air. His Mustangs were P-51B 43-6763 B6-Y *GLAMOROUS GLEN* and P-51Ds 44-13897 B6-Y *GLAMOROUS GLEN II* and 44-14888 B6-Y *GLAMOROUS GLEN III*.

ABOVE: John Kirla's last *SPOOK* was 44-72180 G4-H, which had no victory display. The name was applied in white, outlined with black.

LEFT AND BELOW: Ace Otto Jenkins named P-51D 44-63199 *TOOLIN' FOOLS' REVENGE* in honour of the friends that he had in the ETO. Sadly, Jenkins was killed when this Mustang struck a tree while he was doing an end of tour pass at Leiston on 24 March 1945. The victory symbols were painted in black and the name in yellow.

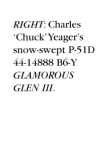

RIGHT: Charles 'Chuck' Yeager's snow-swept P-51D 44-14888 B6-Y *GLAMOROUS GLEN III*.

P-51D-15-NA 44-14888 of the 363rd FS/357th FG, Leiston, January 1945
The third, and last, Mustang assigned to 11.5-kill ace Capt Charles 'Chuck' Yeager, this aircraft was named for his wife. It replaced P-51D 44-13897 in October 1944, and was flown by Yeager until he finished his tour in January 1945. Squadron records reveal that he downed four Fw 190s (on 27 November) and a Me 262 (on 6 November) with this P-51D. The aircraft was then transferred to another pilot and renamed *Melody's Answer*. It was shot down by flak (or possibly by a Bf 109 from JG 301) near Haseloff, in Germany, on 2 March 1945, the 357th FG losing five Mustangs in combat on this day. 44-14888's pilot, Flt Off Patrick L Mallione, was killed.

The other successful 357th FG pilots were:

John A Storch   9 and 5 shared air, 1 and 1 shared ground. P-51B 42-106826 C5-R and P-51Ds 44-13546 C5-R *The Shillelagh* and 44-63164 C5-R *The Shillelagh*

Fletcher E Adams   8 and 2 shared air. P-51B 43-12468 G4-L *Southern Belle* (PoW 30/5/44)

Otto D Jenkins   8 and 1 shared air, 2 ground. P-51B 42-106829 G4-P *Floogie* and P-51Ds 44-14245 G4-P *Floogie II* and 44-63198 G4-X *TOOLIN' FOOL'S REVENGE* (Killed in Flying Accident 24/3/45)

John L Sublett   8 air and 1 ground. P-51D 44-11190 G4-Q *Lady Ovella*

Charles E Weaver   8 air and 3 ground. P-51Ds 44-63779 G4-A and 44-72199 G4-A

BELOW: Charles Weaver had P-51D 44-72199 G4-A marked with an elaborate form of victory symbol that featured a black eagle silhouette holding a swastika.

ABOVE: Also boasting a nude female form, Charles Weaver's unnamed 44-72199 became G4-A after the ace had finished his tour.

Joseph E Broadhead	8 air. P-51B 43-12227 G4-V *Baby Mike* and P-51D 44-14798 G4-V *Master Mike*
Dale E Karger	7 and 1 shared air, 4 ground. P-51Ds 44-15026 C5-U *Cathy Mae* and 44-72313 C5-U *Cathy Mae II*
Robert M Shaw	7 and 2 shared air. P-51D 44-13875 C5-H
Thomas L Hayes	7 and 1 shared air, 2 ground. P-51D 44-13318 C5-N *Frenisi*
Joseph F Pierce	7 air and 1 ground. P-51B 43-6644 B6-N (Killed in Action 21/5/44)
John B Carder	7 air. P-51B 42-106777 C5-J *Taxpayer's Delight* (PoW 12/5/44)
Gerald E Tyler	7 air. P-51B 43-6376 C5-J and P-51D 44-14660 C5-J, both named *Little Duckfoot*
Glennon V Davis	6 and 3 shared air. P-51B 43-6867 C5-O *Pregnant Polecat* (reported Missing in Action 28/4/44 but evaded)
Robert H Becker	6 and 2 shared air. P-51B 42-106783 G4-O *Sebastian* and P-51D 44-13517 G4-O *Sebastian Jr*
James W Browning	6 and 2 shared air. P-51B 43-6563 B6-P and P-51Ds 44-14937 B6-P and 44-72937 B6-P, all named *Gentleman Jim* (Killed in Action 9/2/45)
Gilbert M O'Brien	6 and 2 shared air. P-51B 43-6787 G4-Q *Shanty Irish* and P-51D 44-13719 G4-G
Andrew J Evans	6 air and 2 ground. P-51D 44-64051 G4-B *Little Sweetie 4*
Alva C Murphy	6 air and 2 ground. P-51D 44-13334 G4-U *Bite Me*
John F Pugh	6 air. P-51B 42-106473 G4-N *Geronimo*

ABOVE AND RIGHT:
Dale Karger's 44-15026 C5-U
carried the name *CATHY MAE* on
the left side of the nose and
KARGER'S DOLLIE on the right
side. It was lost with another
pilot on 10 January 1945.

BELOW AND RIGHT: The replacement was 44-72313 *Cathy Mae II*. It is
believed the name was painted in red.

RIGHT: 364th FS P-51D, C5-P. The 'last three' of the fighter's serial had not been repainted on the yellow rudder when this photograph was taken in January 1945.

Robert G Schimanski	5 and 2 shared air, 2 ground. P-51D 44-14334 C5-O
Arval J Roberson	5 and 1 shared air, 1 ground. P-51B 43-6688 G4-A and P-51D 44-13691 G4-A, both named *Passion WAGON*
Paul R Hatala	5 and 1 shared air. P-51D 44-63710 C5-B
William R O'Brien	5 and 1 shared air. P-51D 44-13522 B6-G *Billy's Bitch*
Leroy A Ruder	5 and 1 shared air. P-51B 42-106768 C5-X (Killed in Action 6/6/44)
Robert P Winks	5 and 1 shared air. P-51D 44-13576 C5-W *Trusty Rusty*
Irwin H Dregne	5 air and 5.5 ground. P-51D 44-13408 C5-Q *Ah Fung Goo II* and P-51K 44-11678 C5-Q *Bobby Jeanne/Ah Fung Goo*
Morris A Stanley	5 air and 1.5 ground. P-51D 44-13678 C5-V

ABOVE AND LEFT: Rare colour views of the nude painting that decorated the nose of Arval Roberson's *Passion WAGON* (P-51D 44-13691 G4-A).

Raymond M Bank	5 air. P-51D 44-15266 C5-Y *Fire Ball* (PoW 2/3/45)
Edward W Hiro	5 air. P-51D 44-13518 B6-D *Horse's Itch* (Killed in Action 19/9/44)
Chester K Maxwell	5 air. P-51D 44-63861 C5-H *Lady Eshter*
William C Reese	5 air. P-51B 43-12313 C5-F *Bear River Betsy* (Killed in Action 21/5/44)
Jack R Warren	5 air. P-51B 43-12124 C5-F (Killed in Action 18/3/44)
Frank L Gailer	4 and 3 shared air. P-51C 42-103002 B6-T *Jessil Pessil Mommy* and P-51D 44-11331 B6-A *Expectant* (PoW 27/11/44)
Thomas L Harris	4 air and 2 shared. P-51B 43-6653 C5-S *Lil' Red's Rocket* (PoW 27/5/44)

RIGHT: This flight of four 370th FS P-51Ds is being led by ranking 359th FG ace Capt Ray Wetmore in his 44-14733 CS-L, which he later named on the left side *Daddy's Girl* for his young daughter. The other Mustangs are 44-14521 CS-A *RAYNER Shine*, flown by Lt Col Daniel McKee, 44-14773 CS-G *Mickey the Twist*, flown by Lt Emory Johnson, and 44-14192 CS-S *Blondie II*, flown by Capt Robert McInnes.

359th FG

The most outstanding ace in the 359th FG was Raymond S Wetmore with over 20 victories, of which 16 and two shared were obtained while flying Mustangs. He had previously destroyed four enemy aircraft, and shared in the demise of another, while flying the P-47. Wetmore was also credited with destroying two enemy aircraft and sharing in the destruction of another while strafing. His personal Mustangs were P-51B 42-106894 CS-P, with which he made four of his claims, and P-51D 44-14733 CS-L, which he used to shoot down eight and share in the destruction of two more enemy fighters. The latter P-51D carried the name *Daddy's Girl*. Wetmore was killed in a flying accident in 1951.

Although George A Doersch had a total of 10.5 aerial victories, one of these was obtained while flying a P-47. His assigned P-51C during his first tour was 43-24810 CS-J. Doersch spent his second tour with the 368th FS, where his P-51K was 44-12067 CV-R *OLE' GOAT*.

The 359th FG had seven other pilots who qualified as Mustang aces:

Claude J Crenshaw	7 air and 3 ground. P-51B 42-106689 IV-S and P-51Ds 44-13606 IV-I *LOUISIANA HEAT WAVE* and 44-15016 IV-I *HEATWAVE*
Cyril W Jones	6 air and 5 ground. P-51D 44-14071 CS-W *Dora Dee* (Killed in Action 12/9/44)

BELOW: 359th FG ace George Doersch poses with his P-51D 44-72067 CV-R *OLE' GOAT*, the latter being applied in yellow with black outlining.

David B Archibald	5 air. All with P-51D 44-15555 CV-L on 18/12/44 (PoW on this date too). Previous P-51D 44-14652 CV-L
Niven K Cranfill	5 air. P-51B 42-106848 IV-N *Deviless 2nd* and P-51Ds 44-13390 IV-N *Deviless 3rd*, 44-15100 CV-Q and 44-15717 CV-Q
Ralph L Cox	5 air. P-51Ds 44-14979 CS-H *Little Dixie* and 44-72154 IV-N
Paul E Olson	5 air. All 18/12/44 (PoW on this date too). P-51Bs 42-106917 CV-J *Mari-Helen* and 43-6917 CV-J *Mari-Helen* and P-51D 44-14444 CV-J *Supermouse*
Robert M York	5 air. P-51C 42-103966 CS-K and P-51Ds 44-13966 CS-K and 44-14159 CS-Y *Rudy*

RIGHT: 384th FS ace John Lowell called all his personal aircraft *PENNY*. This was his last P-51D, which bears 17 swastika victory symbols. The fighter's original rudder was repaired or replaced at some point, as the last three (263) of the tail number was missing on the left side and the first three (463) absent from the right side! The strange shaped letter L (for Lowell) on the tail was seen on earlier aircraft in this squadron, suggesting use of the same stencil.

361st FG

Of the six 361st FG Mustang aces, the highest scorer was Dale F Spencer with nine and one shared aerial victories, plus a share in a strafing credit. His assigned aircraft was P-51B 42-106538 E9-S *Little Luke*. William R Beyer also claimed nine aerial kills in P-51s, five of which were shot down in one day, but not with his assigned aircraft, P-51D 44-14144 E9-N.

Urban L Drew had six air and one ground credit with P-51D 44-14164 E2-D *DETROIT Miss*. William T Kemp also had six aerial kills, being assigned P-51C 42-103749 E2-X *Betty Lee* and P-51Ds 44-14 270 E2-X *Betty Lee II* and 44-15076 E2-X *Betty Lee III*.

George R Vanden Heuvel shot down five enemy aircraft and shared another. He also had three ground-strafing credits. His assigned P-51Ds were 44-14685 E9-L and 44-64005 E9-Z, both named *Mary Mine*. The remaining ace was William J Sykes with five air and five ground kills, flying P-51D 44-14520 E9-S. He became a PoW on Christmas Eve 1944.

364th FG

George F Ceullers achieved the highest tally among 364th FG pilots with nine aerial victories. These were in addition to the one and one shared victories he had scored with the Lightning. Ceullers' Mustangs were P-51Ds 44-13971 N2-D, 44-15020 N2-D and 44-72719 N2-D *Constance*.

Ernest E Bankey had eight and a shared aerial victories in Mustangs and one in a Lightning – he also had eight ground strafing claims. Assigned aircraft were P-51Ds 44-13964 5E-B, 44-15019 5E-B *Lucky Lady VI* and 44-73045 5E-B *Lucky Lady VII*.

BELOW: Veteran P-38 pilot Capt Ernest 'Ernie' Bankey was the 364th FG's second-ranking ace in the ETO, flying initially with the 385th FS before moving to the group HQ in December 1944. He increased his score from two to 9.5 aerial kills whilst serving with the HQ, and also claimed eight ground strafing victories. The bulk of his kills came in P-51D 44-15019, although his final two aerial successes were scored in the immaculate *Lucky Lady VII* (44-73045), which appears to have had replacement nose panels recently fitted.

COMBAT REPORT

1st LIEUTENANT URBAN L DREW
375th FS/361st FG
7 October 1944
Time: 1345 hours
Location: Achmer airfield.
Conditions: clear with ground haze.

I was leading Decoy squadron (in P-51D E2-<u>D</u> 44-14164) when I went down to join a fight that was going on under the box of bombers behind our box. When I got there the fight had been dispersed and I could not locate any enemy aircraft. I had left my Red section with the bombers and I had just one flight with me due to a number of previous abortions. I couldn't locate our bombers so I joined up with some red-tailed B-17s that were short on escorting fighters. I stayed with them until I spotted two aircraft on the airfield at Achmer. I watched them for awhile and saw one of them start to taxi. The lead ship was in take-off position on the east-west runway and the taxiing ship got into position for a formation take-off.

I waited until they were both airborne and then I rolled over from 15,000 ft and headed for the attack, with my flight behind me. I caught up with the second Me 262 when he was about 1,000 ft off the ground. I was indicating 450 mph and the jet aircraft could not have been going over 200 mph. I started firing at about 4,000 yards, 30 degrees deflection, and as I closed on him I observed hits all over the wings and fuselage. Just as I passed him I saw a sheet of flame come out near the right wing root. As I glanced back I saw a gigantic explosion and a sheet of red-orange flame shot out over an area of about 1,000 ft.

Six-kill ace 1Lt Urban 'Ben' Drew is helped up onto the wing of his P-51D 44-14164 *DETROIT Miss* by his crew chief, Sgt Vernon Davis, in October 1944. A former flight instructor, Drew completed a solitary tour with the 361st FG's 375th FS. He had the unique distinction of shooting down two Me 262s in a single mission, in this aircraft, on 7 October 1944, this feat being unequalled during World War 2. The seventh kill marking on the canopy rail of *DETROIT Miss* was for Drew's solitary strafing victory (a Ju 52/3m claimed on 16 June 1944).

Ace Urban 'Ben' Drew's *DETROIT Miss* (44-14164 E2-<u>D</u>), with a blue canopy rim carrying his victory scoreboard. The bomb shape on the nose is red and the words yellow.

The other jet aircraft was about 500 yards ahead of me and had started a fast climbing turn to the left. I was still indicating about 400 mph and I had to haul back on the stick to stay with him. I started shooting from about 60 degrees deflection, 300 yards, and my bullets were hitting the tail section of the enemy aircraft. I kept horsing back on the stick and my bullets crept up the fuselage to the cockpit. Just then I saw the canopy go flying off in two sections and the plane rolled over and went into a flat spin. He hit the ground on his back at about a 60-degree angle. I did not see the pilot bale out. The enemy aircraft exploded violently, and as I looked back at the two wrecks there were two mounting columns of black smoke. I claim two Me 262s destroyed.

Ammunition expended: 865 rounds.

P-51D-10-NA 44-14423 of the 434th FS/479th FG, Wattisham, December 1944
Used by 14-kill ace Arthur F Jeffrey as his personal aircraft from September 1944 through
to January 1945, this machine was credited with the destruction of three Fw 190s and a
fourth damaged (all on 5 December 1944) and two Bf 109s destroyed (on 7 October and
2 November 1944). Jeffrey replaced the fighter with P-51K 44-11674, which also carried
the name *BOOMERANG JR.* P-51D 44-14423 was declared salvage in May 1945.

The other 364th FG Mustang aces were:

James M Fowle	8 air, all obtained with P-51D 44-13829 5Y-J *Terry Claire II*. Assigned P-51D 44-14184 5Y-Q *Terry Claire III*
Gilbert L Jamison	7 air. P-51D 44-14035 5E-A *Etta Jane*
Samuel J Wicker	5 air (plus 2 in P-38s). P-51Ds 44-13936 N2-W *Betty Jo III* and 44-14243 N2-W *Betty Jo IV*
James J Pascoe	5 air (plus a shared in a P-38). All victories in P-51D 44-13890 5E-W *Green Eyes*
William F Wilson	5 air. P-51Ds 44-14258 5E-Y and 44-14838 5E-Y (Killed in Flying Accident 1947)

479th FG

The 479th FG's top scorer was Robin Olds with 12 aerial victories in P-51s and five in P-38s.
Olds also had 11 ground strafing credits. His assigned P-51Ds included 44-14426 L2-W
SCAT 5 and 44-72922 L2-W *SCAT VII*. Olds later shot down four MiGs during the Vietnam war.

Arthur F Jeffrey claimed ten aerial victories in P-51s and four in P-38s. His Mustangs,
P-51D 44-14423 L2-O and P-51K 44-11674 L2-O, were both named *BOOMERANG JR.* George
W Gleason had eight aerial victories in Mustangs and three in P-38s. His assigned aircraft was
P-51D 44-14740 L2-H *Hot Toddy*. The fourth 479th FG Mustang ace was Richard G Candelaria
with six aerial victories. He flew P-51K 44-11755 J2-K *My Pride and Joy* and was shot down in
this aircraft and taken prisoner on 13 April 1945.

2nd Scouting Force

The lone 2nd Scouting Force ace was William E Whalen, who claimed five aerial victories with
this unit – three Fw 190s on 26 November 1944 and two Bf 109s (with a third as a probable)
on 9 February 1945. He had also downed a solitary Bf 109 whilst flying with the 4th FG's
334th FS on 18 August 1944. Whalen's Mustang during his time with the latter unit was P-51B
43-6899 QP-O, and his P-51D with the 2nd Scouting Force was 44-14300 WR-A.